The View From the Rectory Window

Father Kenneth S. VanHaverbeke

May your view be blessed!
Father Ken

2

Introduction

Growing up, James Herriot's books about his experience as a veterinarian in post-World War II England fascinated me. He made the daily slogging of a vet's working life seem exciting. The various people and situations he wrote about almost made me want to become a veterinarian. The only real drawback I saw was being around sick animals so much of the time.

Reading Herriot's series "All Creatures Great and Small," helped me to realize that everyone, whether a vet or a cop, a teacher or a businessman, everyone has an intriguing story to tell.

Growing up as a Roman Catholic, I was surrounded by signs of my faith. Not the least being Catholic Priests. "What an interesting combination," I thought, "combining James Herriot's style of storytelling of ordinary life of a vet with the stories a Catholic priest could tell.

At first I thought perhaps because of the much confidentiality a priest must keep, there would be no story to tell. But then remembering the classic "A Diary of a Country Priest," and Brother Benoit's "A view from the monastery," I knew many events of a priest life could be told, and perhaps in doing so, others might understand what a priestly vocation is.

Maybe a young man reading such stories might even be inspired to hear God's call to become a priest, especially since sick animals are not a daily part of priesthood.

What follows are stories of the priesthood. Ordinary, mundane, even boring stories of everyday events: ordinary to a priest that is, but may very well be fascinating to someone who does not live in a collar of black and white.

These were first published in the Diocese of Wichita's Catholic newspaper, The Advance. I am appreciative of the many readers of The Advance who have encouraged me to continue to write about the everyday life of the priesthood. Every day I celebrate Mass and kiss the stole, I thank God for the gift of the priesthood. I am thankful for family, friends, and parishioners to be able to share this gift of the priesthood with them.

Names, dates, and locations have often been changed or altered to protect the privacy of individuals, but join me in looking at the world from a view from the rectory window.

Father Ken VanHaverbeke
Diocese of Wichita

Questions

He was a small boy. A pug nose that was running. His eyes were watery and red. Silently he walked into the sacristy, a variable holy of holies where priest's change into their vestments for the Mass. Once the sacristy was a "male only" domain, but now a grand central station for various people, male and female, altar servers, Eucharistic Ministers, musicians, ushers, and sometimes a lost soul looking for confession or a bathroom. It was into this sacred space Thad came, looking forlorn, as if he had lost his best friend.

In fact, he did. He had only one question. A question that will shake the very depths of any priest worth his salt. A question that requires an answer, but in answering this question, a priest sets his theological foot into murky and sometimes frightening waters. A question of which there is no "right" answers, only an ocean of grey of which the priest is piloting...

With a deep breath, he exhales his question in breath: "Do dogs go to heaven?"

I knew I was on wobbly ground. It seems the most deeply theological questions are asked of me 30 seconds before Mass as I am preparing for the entrance procession. Questions that most certainly deserve an answer, but not in the allotted time given.

What should I do? Tell him of the different souls Saint Thomas Aquinas taught: the 'vegetative soul,' the 'sensitive soul,' and the 'rational soul?' How Saint Thomas would say only humans have a rational soul that will go to heaven, while the other souls will be fulfilled in the beatific vision hence we will have no need for a companion of a pet in heaven because God will fulfill this purpose completely?

Looking beyond Thad, I see my associate: a good, hardworking, young priest, silently shaking his head "no." He and I have already had this discussion. He emphatically believes only rational beings experience the beatific vision of our Lord and I suspect Thad has already gone to my associate, and now is coming to me, the pastor, to receive ex-cathedra, the definitive answer to his question.

In the seminary, a place of formation and education for the priesthood, I remember having conversations at lunch about such questions as whether animals are in heaven.

We would discuss many, many things in the seminary, especially at lunch. Being young, in our twenties, we found these questions fun and stimulating to talk about. A real way of putting to use the theology and philosophy we were ingesting at class.

We discussed questions such as: When did Jesus fully understand He was God? Would Jesus have had a belly-ache? For insofar as He is God, He would have known the fish was old and should have thrown it out, but insofar as He is human, He would not.

'What did the Blessed Virgin Mother know and understand?' was always a good topic of table conversation. Was she the only woman God asked to be the Mother of God?

What if God asked Meltilda the next block over in Nazareth first, and she said "no?" Being conceived without sin did not mean Mary was required to say yes. How did free will come into play in her fiat or yes?

Depending upon a seminarian's view of such questions, we could easily place him in either a "liberal" or "conservative" camp. This was always an important distinction to make. From this knowledge we could speculate who would be selected as a bishop from our class, and whether we would want to serve under him or not. (Secretly every seminarian thinks he could be made bishop someday and in fact every young priest does too!) We were so very young.

Thad did not go away. His demeanor told me he was staying until he got an answer that he understood. Mass would have to wait.

As priests we are expected to know many things: Christology, scripture, canon law, spiritual theology, philosophy, finances, public speaking, good business practices and school or education administration. Our personal and public lives are intertwined having a private life that is public, and a public life that is unique and very knowledgeable in a variety of subjects.

We are expected to give deep, yet pithy homilies while maintaining an engaging liturgical style that would please both readers of the *National Catholic Reporter* and *The Wanderer*. A priest is a man for all seasons, for all peoples, all the time. The expectations are diverse, and yet with time comes wisdom and the realization that our job description is no different than any parent, for in fact that is what we are, a parent...a father.

Looking directly into Thad's watery eyes, I answered as only a parent can: "Yes, Thad, your dog is in heaven with God. All of God's creatures, great and small, return to the loving God that created them, especially those creatures that God created who never sinned against Him."

With a 'humph!' of satisfaction, Thad wheeled out of the sacristy to go to Mass. Following him, I looked up to meet the eyes of my associate. I knew it would an interesting dinner conversation tonight.

"If there are no dogs in Heaven, then when I die I want to go where they went."

-*Will Rogers*

The View

From the rectory's kitchen window I can see the playground. As I was washing my lunch dishes so I could put them into the dishwasher (am I the only one who uses the dishwasher as a purifier, not a washer?), and I noticed a group of four middle school children playing on the playground.

Alone, well after school hours. Playing on the equipment, running around the sign that says, "Adult Supervision Required." I know they are my students, who must have waited patiently, slinking around in the outskirts of the parking lot as if waiting for a ride. A ride they knew wasn't coming. They knew they were to go to "extended day program," but that would mean homework and being with a bunch of little kids. Yuck!

"Oh well," I decided. It's a beautiful day, and they look like they are having fun. No harm....but oops, on a second glance, perhaps they are having too much fun. As a priest for eighteen years, you get an eye for such fun. Now they are running in and out of the school. Another 'oops.' School is over. The school should be locked. How did they get in?

Pebbles, of course, are to be blamed. Whoever was the designer of the landscape and placed rock pebbles around the school building and playground equipment either never had or did not yet have children of their own. These innocent river pebbles are the devil's creation. They are thrown, tossed, and kicked at one another. They are poured down shirts and sometimes the backsides of pants, making the recipient very uncomfortable and seeking revenge. Not exactly what our Lord meant when he said to give the other cheek!

Worse of all, these little demonic pebbles are used by children of God to prop doors open. These clever children knew they could enter the school from the other side of the building, then covertly prop the door open, giving huge access to a game of hide and seek both inside and outside of the school.

With a sigh, I now know what I am required to do as a pastor. If only I didn't look out the window. (Make note: quit looking out the kitchen window.)

Walking over to the playground in a calculated, easy going manner, the children easily saw through my facade to my irritation and they scattered like cats. Tersely calling after them, they looked at me with Bambi eyes and ask me "Huh?!? What!?! We're not doing nothing!" when I asked them why they weren't in extended day.

Remember: they are middle school children; sixth, seventh, or eighth graders. Young enough to have Bambi eyes; old enough to have an attitude. A dangerous combination.

As a young priest before I became pastor, I envisioned the persecution I might endure preaching the Gospel of Jesus Christ. I prayed for the fortitude to do and say what was right and true. Reading and studying the lives of Saint Maximillian Kolbe or the North American martyrs who endured torture and death in bringing the Good News to others, I was spiritually prepared for such persecution.

I was not however prepared for the real world as I would experience it. Never has there been a sleepless night after challenging couples, whether in their twenties or seventies (sin seems to have no age limit) not to commit a sin by living together before entering the sacrament of marriage. Nor do I miss a wink being confronted by a person cursing at me at the gas pump calling me names as a result of well-publicized sins of a few brother priests.

I have trouble getting to sleep after giving a homily about Natural Family Planning and having an entire family stand up and parade out in front of me later telling me I was teaching birth control. Even after having to correct parents for conducting themselves in a most unchristian manner at a football game, I slept like a log.

Preaching the Gospel sometimes is challenging, but it has not been life threatening or a cause of insomnia, but when I feel "un-liked," I lie awake for hours! As priests we are called "father." As a father we must parent, and parenting is not a popularity contest… but as with everyone else, I want to be liked.

Isn't being liked important? St. Francis de Sales wrote sugar will attract more than vinegar. If people don't like me, how can I preach the gospel message? Won't I do more damage to these children's faith by requiring them to call their parents? Will they remember me as the priest who visited their classrooms, heard their confessions, and had them act out the Gospel during the homily?

No, more than likely, they will remember it as they see it: the priest who seemed more concerned about the school building than their souls.

Yet, I do remember reading about a child who was seriously hurt on a playground with no one to help after a seeming innocent fall. I remember the boy who broke his arm while playing football going out for a pass and again, no adult to help. I also know these teens think they are much older and mature by the way they dress, but in fact are young and vulnerable being alone on a playground by themselves.

Oh the fuss they made when I demanded that they go to "extended day". Contrary to the wishes of the children, we called their parents to retrieve their children. Soon dad came and with a puzzled glance toward me asking, "So what was the problem?" After explaining the behavior of the children, the dangers, and the liability of the parish, he gave a shrug and headed for the car with the children.

Perhaps I was overreacting...probably they would have been safe...perhaps I simply didn't like their attitude. As I walked back to the rectory, I knew I could have handled it better. Could have, should have, and hoped I would next time. Then I realized, martyrdom was not just preaching the Gospel, but also caring for His children. All of His children: parent and child, even when you don't do it so well or are misunderstood. Even if they don't like it.

This is martyrdom, this is being a father, and this is being a parish priest: putting the needs of others before your need to be liked.

"THE" Question

For seventeen years I have gone to the same barber. I was taught in the seminary that the relationships a priest make in his first assignment, in his first priestly year, are very important and will be long lasting. This is true of any profession or vocation, I suppose, because of a person's newness and vulnerability. You are open to new experiences and hungry for acceptance. I still have many fond memories and friendships from those first years of priesthood, but I never expected to have such a rapport with a barber shop!

In my case, I think it is less about vulnerability and more about laziness. After four different assignments, some in the same town as the first assignment and some outside, as far as 20 miles away, I still went to the same barber shop. The ease upon which I was able to sit in the chair knowing that Jay or Skip would not beleaguer me with questions about my day, my life, or my hair, but rather would just cut my hair without small talk. It was worth coming back.

Finally that changed. Too far, too much gas, or it was simply time, I don't know, but finally I found myself sitting in a strange barber's chair. A chair where they ask you your name as you enter the store, not to get to know you, but so they can look you up on the computer and see what hair style you like, only to then ask you again how you want it cut once you get settled in the chair.

As soon as I sat down, I knew "THE" question would be coming. After the usual trite questions of: "How are you?"

"Nice weather, but a bit windy out there." "How do you want your hair cut? Cut different from last time?" After all these questions are exhausted, and after a rather stilted pause, "THE" question comes.

I was really rather surprised it wasn't asked earlier. Entering into the national chain barber shop, a young college-aged girl greets me, asks my name, but then becomes impatient with the computer trying to type in my name.

"Oh, JESUS!" she cries out to the computer.

"Yes, Jesus might help in this situation, although Saint Isidore is really the patron saint of computers." I say.

She looks up, sees my Roman collar, turning bright red says, "Oh, God! Oh, I'm sorry, Ohhhh..."

I assure her it's alright, and that perhaps her national chain has divided my last name into two names, thinking the prefix name is my middle name.

Sure enough, there I am in the computer, probably only describing my style of haircut, without mention of the Roman collar.

Getting settled in the chair and after the volley of the usual questions, she finally asks what she really wants to know. She finally asks "THE" question.

"What are you?"

This is not "THE" question, but rather a prelude to "THE" question.

"A priest," I reply. Awkward silence. She is thinking. And not about my hair cut.

"Ohhh" she finally says, and then here it comes, "THE" question:

"So, what do you do?"

There it is! Finally! 'What do you do?' What does a priest do? A straight forward easy question. A good question, but a question where the answer is not so straight forward or easy.

Do I explain what I do in my daily work, or do I explain that priesthood is not so much about accomplishing or doing, but rather about being.

Perhaps a short treatise on Saint John Chrysostom's book *"On the Priesthood"* would be appropriate. Or maybe using an example of a priest she might be familiar with. Maybe Pope John Paul II. But no, I am sure she was probably not even out of grade school when he died.

If I explained what I do, I could tell her what I did just last weekend: celebrated the Sunday Masses; gave a talk about Christian leadership and stewardship; met with a worried mother about her son joining a possible cult in college; anointed a man who was given less than a year to live; grieved with a mother over a miscarriage after 16 weeks; gave a prayer and carefully avoided getting out on the dance floor with our seniors (elders) dance; finally heard the first confessions at a neighboring parish and then back for a blue and gold banquet.

On the other hand maybe that would be a bit too much information and I would never get my hair cut.

Being a priest means we *do* many things: we administrate, minister, parent, teach, study, worry, preach, heal, admonish, clean, employ, pray, preside, and act persona Christa, but explaining what a priest does is like explaining what a mother does, they mother! So I guess that would not help.

Being a priest means we *are* many things: a parent, a teacher, a pupil, a caretaker, a preacher, a healer, a janitor, a pray-er, a Christian, but how can I tell her who I am by telling her it's what I am rather than what I do. Of course that was her first question, 'what are you.'

Sensing my hesitation she tries to rescue me..."Are you the principal of a school or something?"

'Perfect!' I think. "No, but I do teach. I prepare people for sacraments."

"Ohh" she says again...lots of ohh's! I don't think she knows what a sacrament is.

"I do priestly things. Like marriage, baptisms, funerals. You know those sorts of things." I finally say.

"Ohh, that's nice."

"Do you want the back blocked or rounded?" She asks.

"Rounded." I say as I settle deeper into the chair.

I realize I need to have a better answer to "THE" question, or else go back to my old barber who doesn't ask so many questions.

"On the question of relating to our fellowman – our neighbor's spiritual need transcends every commandment. Everything else we do is a means to an end. But love is an end already, since God is love."

-St. Teresia Benedicta (Edith Stein)

20

Clerics

It is said that everyone loves a man in a uniform.

I remember the first uniform I wore. It wasn't really a uniform, more of a dress code. Actually reflecting back, I probably looked more like Herb Tarlek, that obnoxious and wildly dressed character in WKRP, a 1970's television sitcom. Mine was the uniform of a grocery store sacker. Yes, there was a time when young men would sack your groceries and even carry them out to the car.

It was while wearing this uniform I experienced the frustration of following a woman, circling the parking lot searching for her car, only for her to realize that we were looking for the wrong car. She had driven her husband's car, which we eventually found parked next to the front door of the store!

My uniform for such parking lot adventures were blue jeans, a dress shirt, and a very wide tie that I borrowed from my father's closet. This was the '70's so of course the tie was earth toned and wide striped, in a combination of oranges' and browns'. This was my first experience of wearing a uniform.

After graduating from college and many uniforms later, I began my seminary formation and put on yet another uniform of sorts: clerical garb or clerics of black and white.

Distinct clothing for priests was not adopted in the early centuries of the church. In fact Pope Celestine in 428 wrote to bishops in Gaul rebuking them for wearing clothing which made them conspicuous. He said "we [the bishops and clergy] should be distinguished from the common people by our learning, not by our clothes; by our conduct, not by our dress; by cleanness of mind, not by the care we spend upon our person" (Mansi, "Concilia", IV, 465).

This however soon changed when Roman citizens would later begin to change their clothing habits in the 6th century when the clergy continued to wear the older style of clothing which was a long tunic and cloak, representing the toga, and the laity began to wear a short tunic with breeches and mantle.

Most religious "habits" or garbs were simply an older fashion of the people of that time. For instance if you see a priest with a chasuble you probably would not realize that in the day of Bishop Patrick (Saint Patrick) he and the priests adopted this dress because it was the clothing of the poor. Of course Mother Teresa's blue and white garb was also the common clothing of the people living in Calcutta.

With none of this in mind, I had a mixed bag of feelings the first time I put on clerics, the black pants, shirt, and white collar after arriving at the seminary. There we were, about six of us young seminarians in our twenties, after having donned our new attire, standing in the large common bathroom, looking at ourselves in the mirrors, laughing, poking fun at each other, feeling very much out of place and yet secretly both pleased and nervous.

I did not fully understand then but clerics are a sign of reality and hope, as is a parish priest: the reality of death and the hope of eternal life and death; reality of sin and the hope of God's love for the sinner; reality of heaven uniting with earth.

Every Ash Wednesday Christians throughout the world put on the black and white of the cleric, ashes. The priest or minister says: "Remember you are dust, and to dust you shall return." The black and white a priest wears reminds us of the reality of death, sin, and that Adam was made from the dust of the earth. The black and white also reminds us of the hope of eternal life, the realization of God's love for us, and Emmanuel, i.e., God among us!

A priest knows he has truly integrated his priesthood into his Christian life when his black and white clerics become so much a part of him, he doesn't realize if he is, or is not wearing them. Just as a Christian knows he or she is truly integrated Christian when people look at them and see Christ: they know us by our love.

I remember the first few years of priesthood anticipating my "day off." A day away from the rectory, away from probing questions of staff or housekeeper, away from the pastor, just AWAY! I would get into my blue jeans and tee shirt; breathe a deep sigh of relief and think, "Now! I can be just me!"

Years later, after many "days off" and even more days "on," I ceased to see any difference between my outer self from my inner self. I knew I arrived at this point when I would go to the grocery store and parishioners would not recognize me.

"That's funny" I would think, "why didn't Mrs. So and So say something to me?"

Then at the check-out line she would look up with recognition and say,

"Oh Father, I didn't recognize you out of uniform!"

I would look down, suddenly realizing I was not in my black and white clerics.

Or when I would go into a restaurant and everyone would stare at me. I would coyly look down to make certain my pants zipper was appropriately up, and suddenly realize, "Ohhh, I'm wearing clerics...that's why they are staring!"

Whether I am in clerics or out jogging in my sweat pants and shirt, I am a priest, through and through.

Wearing my black and white clerics can bring me a lot of attention. In order to gain the attention of any grade school crowd, furiously eating their lunch and talking, all I have to do is walk through the cafeteria with clerics, and every little hand is waving, trying to grab the attention of "Father!" For them, my clerics are a sign of love of which they want.

I remember another time in a restaurant sitting in a booth. I could see that the man and woman next to my booth were distracted by my presence. The man kept glancing back at me. Finally he got up the nerve and asked,

"Just *WHAT* are you?!?"

I was taken aback, until again, I realized I was wearing my clerics which was the cause his question.

"I am a Catholic priest."

"Oh." He said. "I figured you were something."

Yes, I thought, I *am* something. I am a sign of the reality of sin and death, and I am a visible reminder of Jesus Christ who has brought us the hope of forgiveness and eternal life. Yes, I am a priest.

I understand what Pope Celestine was getting at in 428. There is always a danger when wearing a uniform, badge, or clerics to become self-righteous or vain. Clerics or a uniform doesn't have to make you conspicuous, drawing attention to self, but when approached with humility accompanied by a life of charity and service, a uniform, such as clerics can simply be an instrument of the Lord, allowing both the wearer and the observer to experience a visible presence of our God in a fragile world.

An Agent of Conversion and Vocation

The stop sign was a glowing red. I remember it vividly. The day was extremely sunny, the February air was crisp and winter had not yet relinquished its hold on the earth, but I had just relinquished myself to God. I always knew I would, but didn't know the when or the how.

The day was in 1986. I was in Manhattan, Kansas, driving back to the rental house that I shared with three other boys while attending my final year at Kansas State University. I was returning from an appointment at Seven Dolores Parish. At that time, I didn't know a "dolor" from a "dollar!" (dolor is Latin for sorrow) I had met with the parish priest to find out what I needed to do to enter the seminary.

The stop sign was memorable, because for the previous six or so blocks before it, I was on "cloud nine" realizing I was finally responding to a call that I had heard for many years.

It was at the stop sign all that changed and I suddenly thought, "What did I just do!!!"

The gravity of what I was being open to left me overwhelmed. I went home that night among my friends, not sure of what to do next. The priest said that I should simply continue to live my college life and then prepare for seminary. It would come soon enough and so just enjoy the last few months of college.

I tried, but it was different. Now I had a purpose. Now I had a goal. Now I was finally answering "The Call" that had rumbled in my heart since third grade. I felt like Saint Paul after his conversion event, being led by the hand to Ananias in Damascus to learn about Jesus. (Acts 9:8) It was a turning point for me.

It was in my first semester of the seminary that the feeling be being overwhelmed left me and I knew I was on the correct path. Throughout the seminary formation, I paced myself one semester at a time, ending each semester with the question for God and self: "Do I continue?" The answer in my heart was always "Yes, but only if you also desire it!"

Conversion or compunction, is an event which leads to a spiritual awakening. For some this event is sudden, but for others it is gradual. For all, it is a turning point.

Conversion has been described as a "pricking." Our conscience is pricked: perhaps by a shameful past, or perhaps by discontent with our present life, or by a fervent desire for a different life. The conversion moment is very strong and subdues our natural tendency to remain status quo. It changes us.

God always gives us freedom to accept conversion or reject it, and so if we allow it, this conversion will now begin to influence our daily actions and lives. It becomes a conversatio (way of life).

My conversion continued, and it wasn't until Bishop Gerber laid his hands upon me at ordination May 25th of 1991 that my "compunctio" was confirmed and affirmed by the church, but it didn't end there!

Conversion is not a onetime event. Throughout my priesthood I've had experiences and events that have humbled and continued to convert me in my acting or thinking, because even though we have been converted, we also can become forgetful. Negligence, sloth, complacency are all thief's of the night which can steal away our spiritual lives leaving us quite empty. (1 Peter 5:8)

As a priest though, I not only experience my ongoing conversion, but I am also an agent of conversion and vocation for others. We are not "secret" agents, but sometimes God works clandestinely through us!

One notable conversion is fresh in my memory. Joseph was an energetic and ornery fifth grader. If there is one thing I've learned as a priest is that if a boy is ornery, keep him close by. Such a boy can go either way becoming a saint or an outlaw. So anytime I needed a server or help in the church, I would make sure Joseph was included. The only drawback is that Joseph wasn't Catholic.

Perhaps I should not have included Joseph but my pastoral sense told me to keep him active and close at hand, even serving at the Mass. It is unusual for a non-Catholic to be allowed to serve Mass but he was most respectful and awed by the whole ritual. By serving and being around the other children in our Catholic grade school, he asked lots of questions and became very curious about the Catholic way of life.

As I was leaving Mass one cold wintery night, Joseph breathlessly ran after me, yelling at the top of his voice,

"Father! I want to become Catholic!"

The glow on his face, the sparkle of enthusiasm in his eyes were not just from the cold air and from running after me, it was conversion and vocation. He was responding to a call God placed in his heart. A call that I was able to cultivate for the Lord. I brought Joseph into the church that Easter and he received his First Holy Communion.

I have since left that parish but often think of young Joseph who by now is a young adult. It is my hope that his conversion has continued.

This is what it means to be a priest: planting seeds and then allowing God or perhaps another pastor to cultivate them, allowing God to continue conversion in me and being an element on other's conversion.

I remember that stop sign well and I am so glad I did in fact, stop my truck for traffic but did not stop the conversion that was occurring in my heart, so that I could continue and be a priest, an agent of conversion and vocation.

Therefore, stay awake, for you do not know on what day your Lord is coming.

-The Gospel of Matthew 24:42

Community Life

The note came by way of an amused secretary carrying a small folded piece of paper. A note from Devon. Devon was a dark headed second grader who always had a ready smile and an equally ready question. Today, his question was written and I could feel his smile in his words as I read it.

"Dear Father Ken," it began. A good start because my last name has twelve letters in it so most of the children and parishioners never quite get my whole name. My first name is a bit easier, but even then I am still often called by my associate's name, unless of course there is a complaint! Then I try to pass myself off for the associate. Doesn't always work.

The note read:
> "Dear Father Ken,
> I am a second grader.
> I have a question.
> How come the third week of Advent is pink?
> Wait there's more.
> I want to be a alter server when I grow up.
> I hope that I don't forget you when I grow up.
> You and Father are a nice pair.
> Sincerely,
> Yours truly,
> Your friend,
> Devon"

What Devon did the majority of Catholics do; not misspelling "altar" with "alter," which the majority of Catholics actually do. No what he did was: watch priests!

In the seminary we were taught after ordination as priests we would live in a "fish bowl." Often I have observed that it feels more like an ancient ships "crow's nest." Before sonar and radar, a ships crow's nest was a perch high above the deck of the ship where a sailor would be looking across the vastness of the ocean and preventing the ship from running aground or into another ship. As a priest, I often feel like that sailor in the crow's nest especially when a parishioner would say in the morning, "Saw your light on late last night. Hospital call or a good television show?"

Being a priest means I am very visible. A priest's mannerisms, his recreation, even the food he eats will be seen by his parishioners. Going to the grocery store is an adventure. First, the reaction of the children whispering to their parents in that ever so soft voice that can be heard throughout the store and the look of utter amazement of seeing Father shopping and realizing that Father eats!

"Look! There's Father!!!" They exclaim!

Then the reactions of the adults during the usual conversation of "Hi" "how are you?" "Cold/warm outside," it is during these conversations the parishioner takes quick downward glances at what is in the shopping cart, wondering what *does* Father really eat. I can see them thinking: 'Looks like a lot of ice cream!' …'I wonder why he is buying so much oatmeal?...probably to balance out the ice cream!'

The children are often much bolder and will snoop through the basket making observations: "You sure like potato chips! My mom won't let me eat those! Deodorant? My grandpa uses that kind!"

Being so visible is also a great advantage in proclaiming the joy of the Gospel. In Devon's observation of me; he picked up on one very important matter that Catholics like to observe: how does a priest get along with his brother priests?

Living in community is hard work. Being married and the union of two wills is so difficult that our Lord has given us sacramental grace in order to live it out. Family life that is so central to the life and health of the Church is not always pretty. The pettiness, the jealousies, even fights over the bathroom can leave many a person desiring to become a hermit. Community life and family life is hard work.

Therefore, parishes that have more than one priest; have the opportunity to see if the priests practice what they preach! It is good for both the parish and the priests.

Living with another priest is both a joy and an inconvenience. A joy in having someone to share a meal, to enjoy a television show, a conversation, and to work with. An inconvenience because we probably did not know each other prior to living and working together and living with your boss is not easy, especially if he has a pet!

And then there is the generation gap. Most parishes with two or more priests have an older priest and a newly ordained priest. I never thought of myself as being old until I began discussing a television show of the 1970's and my associate gave me that quizzical look. I realized he was still a toddler and perhaps not yet born when the show aired!

Our differences in ages, personality, family backgrounds affect the way we pastor, the way we communicate, the way we live. Ahh, community life!

Saint Paul wrote to a young priest by the name of Timothy two letters. In the second letter, Paul gives Timothy some very practical advice: "be strong in the grace that is in Christ Jesus...bear your share of hardship along with me..." (2Timothy 1)

These words express why priests need priests. It is difficult to live such a visible life. Lives where your words and actions can either soothe or hurt, heal or condemn, preach the Gospel or scandalize. Priests need priests to bear with each other and for each other the hardships of authentically proclaiming the Good News of Jesus.

Why is the third candle pink Devon? Because we remember in the midst of waiting for the Lord there are sorrows and hardships, but in the midst of these hardships there is still joy!

I am so glad Devon could see that my associate and I make a "nice pair," for Jesus sent us out two by two, not one by one.(Luke 10:1) In preaching the Gospel and living with another priest, our lives can be a joy, perhaps visibly showing the "good" in the Good News of Jesus! This I hope all the "Devon's" whom I have served in the past won't forget when they grow up!

Aftermath and Emptiness

The church is still now. The afternoon sun creates shafts of light through the stained glass windows and dust particles are sparkling in the sun light. Hard to believe just thirty minutes ago the church was crammed with parents, children, elderly, parishioners and visitors. Perfume and cologne still lingered in the air, as well as the occasional Cheerios on the floor.

It is Christmas, and the Masses are over. The masses of people have left, leaving the church empty. This is an emptiness that can either mock or embrace you. It is an emptiness that can be quickly filled with activities or filled with quiet gratitude of the Lord's presence.

In my first year as an ordained priest I learned the meaning of this emptiness. That first year was filled with so many "firsts." The first time I heard a confession or the first grade school graduation (and the first pre-school graduation which I really don't understand). The first time I anointed a person. The first time I was scolded by a parishioner for something I said. The first time I helped and ministered to a person and was present when they entered into eternal life. The year of the firsts!

Of all these firsts, my first Christmas as a priest is prominent in my memory. That Advent was such a whirlwind of activity: confessions, school plays, confessions, school band concerts, school confessions, school faculty party, and then of course there were the lots of confessions!

One of the more important duties for Advent, as you see, is celebrating the sacrament of Confession. A wise old retired priest recently commented to me that perhaps we have been wrong by promoting Advent and Lenten confessions so much. Not that these seasons of preparation, fasting, and penance are not excellent times to celebrate the sacrament of Confession, but by having such an emphasis on Confession in these two seasons, we might be giving the impression that they are the only seasons to go to confession!

School children, high school students and parishioners are all important to hear confessions, but the homebound and those in nursing homes are most special. In large parishes the homebound are often served by the associate priest. This allows the newly ordained priest to get to know this very important segment of the parish in a special way and to create relationships, which are sometimes short term. Often times the newly ordained are assigned the youth ministry so visiting the homebound provides a good balance and experience.

This was the case in my first Advent. On my rounds was a man who was dying of cancer. He was a young man, perhaps in his forties, with a wife and three children. As I would regularly visit him and prepare him for the celebration of Christmas, I had an idea I was also preparing him for eternal life.

We would talk about his past, his dreams of the future and his present illness, all the while knowing it was the present illness that was making him reflect on the past and realize that his future would not be on earth.

It was humbling to be so accepted by the family for a short, yet very intense time. I became such a regular that I no longer needed to call before I came and would simply let myself into the house and go directly to his bedside. I was one of them.

In our conversations we would read the scriptural passages about what heaven would be like: 'the kingdom of God is like a mustard seed...' or 'the kingdom of heaven is like a merchant who when finding a pearl of great price goes and sells all that he has...' These passages gave us a springboard to prayer and allowed the family to participate.

Our conversations as Christmas drew near were shorter because of the pain medication necessary for him to take. Fading in and out, his primary concern at the end was not his pain, nor regret of anything of his past for that had already been resolved through the sacraments; no his primary concern now was that his wife and children would be cared for by family and the parish.

There is a painting by Rembrandt called of The Prodigal Son. If you look at this beautiful painting of which Henri Nouwen wrote an exceptional book about, you will see a very intimate scene of a father welcoming his wayward prodigal son, and the older brother looking on. If you look closely, you will see another person in the upper left corner of the scene. This person is neither in the light nor in the forefront but still very much part of the scene. This, I have often thought, visually portrays a priest.

Very often a priest is part of such intense and intimate moments of parishioner's lives. We are there to support, journey with, and to bring the presence of Jesus to times of hurt and healing. We are invited to many such intimate moments, but afterwards the family moves on, and the priest remains for another family or for another time.

Soon after Christmas my friend, for that is what we had become, entered into eternal life. Abruptly my schedule changed and no longer would I daily drop by the house, no longer would I let myself in to pray or to bring the Eucharist to the family, no longer was I as close to the family.

The family remained in the parish; I remained their priest for many years until I was transferred. We remained friends, but it was different. Occasionally I meet the children as they have grown, married, and have become Catholic adults. What a joy it is to see them continuing their Catholic faith but there remains an emptiness.

An emptiness where a person once was; an emptiness of what once was done and no longer will be; an emptiness that will not be filled. An emptiness that can either embrace you or mock you. It is an emptiness that can be quickly filled with activities or filled with quiet gratitude of the Lord's presence.

As a priest, sometimes I run from this emptiness and I try to fill it with activity, but more often than naught it is in an empty church on a Christmas afternoon that you will find me...waiting; for it was in emptiness that God finds us!

Wisdom. When to, when not to.

Perhaps it was the manner in which they approached in their teenage swagger. Perhaps it was the nervous glancing around. Whatever it was, as I looked out the rectory kitchen window, three young men caught my eye and I knew they were up to no good.

Parents have this. Teachers develop it. Priests, especially pastors have this capability. It's an intuition that something is amiss, or the "eyes in the back of the head" condition. Sometimes such ability can be helpful, sometimes I just lower my eyes and think, "What 'Father' doesn't know, won't hurt." Because when 'Father" *does* know, he has to do something. Wisdom and knowledge are two different things. Knowledge can be learned, but wisdom is the application of that knowledge. Wisdom is knowing when to act on knowledge and when not to.

A priest must be knowledgeable on many things: prayer, spirituality, business practices, employment issues, church history, canon law, the liturgy, but more importantly a priest must be a man of wisdom. One of my favorite prayers that I pray daily is the Serenity Prayer. "God grant me the serenity to accept the things I cannot change, the courage to change the things I can, and the wisdom to know the different." It is the practice of wisdom that can make a priest's life or anybody's life either serene or extremely difficult.

Jesus was a pastor and was faced with such challenges. In the Gospel of John, Jesus announces to the Apostles that "one of you will betray me." (Jn 13:21) Who was He talking about? Judas is who we naturally think, and of course Judas does betray him, but what about Peter? In the same chapter Jesus predicts Peter's betrayal. (Jn 13:36-38).

Jesus has knowledge of what His followers are capable of doing and are going to be doing. Does He intervene? Does He placidly sit aside? He changed what He could, i.e., He announced and predicted what would happen, allowing both Judas and Peter to turn aside and make a different decision. But most wisely, Jesus accepted that which He could not change, i.e., the free will of these men and their decisions.

Every parish I've served, I've had the privilege of having a Catholic school and have worked side by side with some of the finest Catholic educators in the country. They are so dedicated that sometimes they make the erroneous decision to come up to the school and work on Sunday's in spite of God's commandment to 'keep holy the Sabbath.'

I've encouraged them to give good example and keep Sunday as a day of rest. Once I point out the necessity of a day of rest and how giving such a good example to the rest of the parish is important, the teachers very willing complied.

Everyone that is, except Marge (name has been changed to protect the innocent...me!) Marge was so worried about having everything ready for school on Monday she would sneak into the school building to get some last minute preparations for her class on Sunday afternoon or evening. She would go so far as to park down the street and walk a block to the school so I wouldn't see her car in the church parking lot on a Sunday afternoon.

When I first realized what was going on, my emotions would get the better of me and I would think, "How dare she? I told her not to do that! I'm the boss...she has to do what I say!"

Then wisdom takes over. I can't force another to do what I think is right. No, being a pastor has taught me to try to see through the eyes of Christ. Christ taught us the right way to live, but He also allowed us to then make our own decisions and was there even after we made the wrong decision. (See John 21 15-19 for an example)

The greatest act of love one can give to another is to allow another person to sin against you! Now Marge working on a Sunday afternoon after I asked her not to is not by any means a grave sin, but it does show a willful disregard. And that is what sin is, a willful disregard.

Again, the greatest act of love one can give to another is to allow another person to sin against you. Sound radical? Absurd? "But I say to you offer no resistance to one who is evil. When someone strikes you on your right cheek, turn and offer the other to him as well..." (Matthew 5: 39) Radical yes, but straight from the words of Jesus.

Being a pastor, a priest, a teacher, parent, anyone in a leadership position must be a person of wisdom, knowing when to act and when not to act. Acting with wisdom allows serenity into one's life.

My boys I saw out the window? Well, I decided as I looked out the window that they were in fact up to no good, but I also knew they couldn't get into too much trouble...perhaps throwing rocks, sneaking a smoke, or jumping on playground equipment made for children half their size and weight.

Comfortable with that decision, I looked away from the window for but a moment. As I looked out the window moments later, I saw a three foot flame engulfing the base of the teeter totter. Wisely I revised my previous decision and as quickly as I could, ran to see what they were up to. By the time I arrived, the flame was smoldering and going out.

"Huh, what do you mean? We aren't doing anything!" was the response I received when I breathlessly asked (perhaps yelled) "What are you doing???" When I pointed to the smoldering mass of something at the base of the teeter totter, one boy sheepishly responded, "Well...we were just seeing if a ping pong ball would catch fire."

"Does it?" I surprised them by asking.

"Sure does! Huge flame! Must have some combustible chemicals in it!" he responded.

After thinking I could call the police, call their parents, or angrily kick them off the property, I wisely responded: "Okay boys, be careful you don't burn down my church."

"Okay, Father! I can see how that might be a concern. We won't do it again." He said. A wise decision indeed.

Wisdom. Knowing when and when not to act on knowledge.

Changes of Assignment Part One: Leaving

Never! They never were weeping loudly or threw their arms around me, kissing me! But that is what they did to Saint Paul when he left their community!

After Easter and before Pentecost, readings at Mass are taken from the Acts of the Apostles. The weeping and kissing was the result of Saint Paul's farewell speech at Miletus (20:17-35). This reading is appropriate at this time of the year with the many transitions occurring: graduations, the school year's end, and the change of assignments for parish priests.

Saint Paul's heartfelt discourse speaks how he is "compelled by the Spirit" to leave. His future is uncertain but his priority is the proclamation of the Gospel: "I consider life of no importance to me, if only I may finish my course and the ministry that I received from the Lord Jesus, to bear witness to the gospel of God's grace." (20:24)

The thoughts and feelings Saint Paul conveyed are those of a priest changing assignments.

The feelings of moving from one parish to another are confusing for a priest. Within one day you feel loss, then excitement, then disorientation. The emotions of the parish are also chaotic. "Why are 'they' moving him? Who are we getting? What does it all mean?"

Knowing this what can we do? Priests, like everyone, often go to extremes. The two extremes for a priest in leaving takes on two natures: either they never seem to go away, i.e., the Going Away Party that never seems to go away! Or poof! They are gone in the middle of the night. Both extremes are to be avoided.

The Church encourages what is described as "deliberate leave-taking." This recognizes a transition as a holy event. It creates room for the Holy Spirit to be felt. The final discourse recorded by Saint John shows us how Jesus was deliberate in his leave-taking (John 14-17) and provides a good example.

There are several steps in deliberate leave-taking. First, the good byes. A priest once told me 'Life is a series of hellos and goodbyes.' Taking the time to face people directly, assuring them of prayer, and thanking them for their love and support are vital. Often because goodbyes are painful, this obvious step is overlooked or postponed until it is too late.

Another overlooked step in leave-taking is reconciliation. Letting go of past hurts or trying to resolve past differences can be disregarded because "I'm leaving anyway!" When a person leaves, there is a wonderful opportunity for healing because of the very fact of the impending separation. Perhaps the conflict cannot be resolved, but the healing may come in the form of acknowledging the differences and wishing each other the best for the future. Ignoring this step can have a negative impact on future relationships.

Frank (name has been changed, so don't even try to figure it out!) was a person who I never seemed to satisfy. He was a very good man, but would often expect things out of me that I knew I could not do. When it came time for me to leave, he was the first person to wish me well in my new assignment.

Perhaps he was thinking, 'Good riddance!' but I believe he genuinely cared for me, and my going away provided him the opportunity to show this in spite of his opinion of me. (I am also pretty sure he was one of the first to beat a path to the new pastor's door!)

Expressed gratitude is the final step in deliberate leave-taking. When a priest expresses his gratitude to a parish, he recognizes how important the People of God were to him in allowing him to be their spiritual father. When a parish expresses gratitude to the departing priest, they recognize more than the gifts of that particular priest, they give God and the Church thanks for the stability of the Church. Even though their pastor is leaving, another is there to step in, normally the same day!

This leave-taking should take some ritualized form; perhaps a final Mass, dinner, etc. These steps allow for both priest and parish to experience the joy and sorrow of the transition.

What to give a priest who is leaving? Most of all prayers. Remember, he is packing all of his belongings and we priests generally travel light, so additional mementos although well meaning, are not always fully appreciated.

Also, when it's announced that a priest is leaving, he is deluged with many invitations for dinner or get-togethers. Be gracious in understanding that he might not be able or willing to accept the invitation; allow him some wiggle room to decline. That being said, the invitation might be welcomed by the priest because of the busyness of the event and the need to get away for a moment.

One of the greatest gifts in transition I received was a small 3 x 5" notebook where parishioners wrote down a particular Gospel message, homily point, or adage of mine. It took me several months before I was ready to sit down and read what they said of me, but seeing they remembered something I said was a true gift.

Perhaps in the same vein, written notes of how that priest made a difference in the parish or the lives of the parishioners. Or knowing where the priest is going, gift certificates to a local restaurant or business. Even a gas card would be great for a priest who would be doing some driving at his next assignment!

One time I asked an older priest why we priests seem to talk about 'Who was going where' every time priests gathered. He said we are like the Israelites in the desert who only talked about food and leadership because food and where they were being led was their life. We talk about our assignments so much because the people whom we serve are our life!

Transitions are a challenging task for both priest and parish because the relationship between a priest and his flock is so significant, but we wouldn't want it any other way, would we?

And while my former parishioners didn't 'weep loudly, throwing their arms around my neck kissing me,' I know I was appreciated, loved, and accepted... and would be at my next assignment too!

Changes of Assignment: Receiving a New Pastor

He was waiting for me. I was sure of it. People waiting for the new pastor have a certain look. Often times it's a look of: "Who are you replacing our beloved pastor?" Or it can be a look of: "Finally, now maybe this new priest will ...."

Amid the chaos of people moving boxes, introducing themselves, and cleaning out space for more boxes, a little man sat in the corner of the rectory office watching it all. But most of all, he was eyeing me.

I was new to the parish. That morning I woke up in the bedroom that I had woke up in for many years; celebrated Mass with a community that I had served for many years; and handed over a familiar set of keys to the secretary knowing I would never use them again. It all seemed like a blur.

Arriving at the new parish, I was welcomed by a group of parishioners waiting for me. What a pleasant surprise! My former parishioners ("former" by about one hour) who were helping me move introduced themselves and then they all got to work.

It took all of five minutes. Without furniture, household goods, or bulky possessions and with many hands, moving a priest is fairly easy. Books and clothes make up most of our possessions. After the initial rush of boxes, the stacking in the corner of the bedroom, my former and new parishioners ("new" by about ten minutes) take their leave for me to unpack in privacy.

I am alone...except for the little man in the corner of the office still watching me.

I know I need to see what I can do for him, but I am hesitant to begin. The first surge of parishioners in a new parish can often be challenging because often they have "beaten a path" to my door either wanting something the former pastor would not give them, or with a suggestion.

The stability of the Church is a gift from God. When one parish priest leaves, another comes. (Please pray for vocations, encourage your young men to become priests so this gift continues! What a wonderful life it is!) Coming to a new parish for a priest is barraged with newness: new parish, new family community, new surroundings, new church building, new faces, new names, and in many ways, a new job.

No wonder one of my seminary professors said with all that newness get your priorities straight: know where all the bathrooms are! Even those are new to you! Taking the place of a brother priest is daunting. You want to be yourself, but you can't help but compare yourself to what you perceive the other pastor to be. Sometimes you replace a brother priest who seemed to walk on water in your eyes, only not to give you a map detailing where the rocks are beneath the surface.

Or you replace a brother priest who had to make some difficult and unpopular decisions. Then you can catch yourself trying to be everyone's friend, not wanting to offend anyone and wanting to be known as "the nice guy."

Compare, competition, and complaining are the three cancers for a priest. We sometimes find ourselves comparing our ministry or parish with that of another priest, competing for popularity, and complaining about our assignment, authority, or brother priest. A deadly disease these three "C's." A disease that deadens a priestly heart.

I decide to get my priorities straight. I first go to the Church for a prayer (subsequent to finding the restroom!). After a short prayer of thanksgiving before the Eucharist, *"wondering thoughts"* begin to distract me. Thoughts such as: "I *wonder* why it is so cold in this church. I *wonder* who is responsible for setting the temperature. I *wonder* who trains the altar servers. I *wonder* what the story is behind that beautiful statue. How in the *wonder* do you get a casket down this aisle?

Giving up on any real deep prayer experience, I *wonder* back to the rectory.

"What's this?" I think. On the kitchen table is a candy bouquet (much more practical than flowers!) and a basket of food.

The candy bouquet was sent by some former parishioners wishing me well in my new assignment. I'll put it with a 'care package' of comfort food munchies my former staff gave me when I was leaving.

The basket from the new parish's Altar Society and was filled with some easy to prepare food items and homemade chicken and noodles. Perfect for dinner tonight! Now I won't have to go the grocery story immediately and replace all the rice cakes and low salt (read no-taste) soups in the pantry left by the former heart healthy conscious pastor.

Returning back to the rectory office I suddenly remember the little man in the corner. He was busily talking to my new secretary, whose name I keep getting confused with the school secretary. Not a good start!

When he sees me, he gets up and walks across the room. "I didn't want to disturb you before Father, knowing this was your first day here, and I know you are busy getting settled. I was here getting a Mass said for my wife who passed away this time last year."

Then he went on to say, "Father *'Former Pastor'* was such a gift to me during that time...."

Oh, here it comes, I thought.... 'You got pretty big shoes to fill" or "I think you should consider..." I've heard them both on my first day at a new parish.

But how little faith I have...for he went on to say,... "and I look forward to the gifts you bring to our parish too. Welcome! We are glad you are here!"

Suddenly, I was glad that I was there too!

1. Be patient with him. The stress of moving, the grief of leaving a familiar parish and the newness of it all might be a bit much for him. Be patient.

2. Don't beat a path to his door. Give him some time to unpack, get settled, finding all the bathrooms and getting the secretary's names straight. This might take a month or two, or longer...see #1.

3. Tell him your name and what you are involved with. Don't do this once or twice, but a number of times. Don't be offended if in six months or a year later he doesn't remember your name. He wants too. Really! So don't embarrass him, tell him again!

4. Make sure he has help moving in if he wants it. The parish secretary can help knowing if he needs help. Some priests would welcome help, others desire privacy. We are all different. A nice welcome basket from the Altar Society or Knights of Columbus is always thoughtful.

5. Let him change his mind! Sometimes a decision made early is rushed or made without fully understanding the situation. It might be necessary for him to change his mind. Give him some wiggle room.

6. Try not to compare him to your former pastor. This will not be fully possible of course, and he will struggle in comparing his previous parish to the present. Comparisons will only impede a relationship.

7. Tell him your story, the story of the parish, the traditions, and the important values of the parish. Every parish and tradition in a parish has a story behind it. These stories are important for him to know.

8. When he asks how something is done in the past or what the protocol is, refrain from telling him "Whatever you would like Father!" We generally want to keep things the way they are and not fix something that is not broken, so don't be afraid to tell him how things operate in the parish. Sometimes a new pastor makes changes without even knowing they have changed anything because no one told him.

9. Let him get to know you and the parish. Be sure to invite him to different parish events. Yes, he sees the bulletin and should know when something is happening but he might not know if he is really wanted.

10. Pray for him and let him know you are praying for him!

Newly Ordained Humility

It is interesting how I remember the time of day of certain events. One event I vividly remember is a Monday afternoon at 2pm. Three weeks prior to this Monday afternoon, I had lain prostrate on green carpet in the Cathedral, rising to receive the bishop's hands on my head, ordaining me to the priesthood of Jesus Christ and receiving oil on my hands to baptize, consecrate, and forgive. Those bishop's hands would later pen a letter to me, assigning me to a parish, arriving on a Monday afternoon at 2pm - my first parish.

In many ways, those hands of my bishop both gently pushed me and firmly led me by the hand to my first assignment. Only three things did I request of God in the seminary while praying about my first assignment: 1) Please don't send me to replace a priest that was very dynamic and popular; 2) Please don't make me responsible for building a church; 3) And, please give me a pastor who is patient and kind.

Only the third request was heard. I have since learned not to tell God what to do in assigning me for God answers all your prayers, but rarely in the manner that you outline for Him. Coming to a parish for the first time that Monday afternoon at 2pm, I walked into a new community, a new job, a new part of town, a new house, and a new life. It was so overwhelming that I did not realize how overwhelming it was until much later.

My new pastor arrived two hours after I did. The poor man never had an associate before...don't think he has had once since! Not entirely sure what to do with an "associate", he, instead of treating me like a "wet behind the ears" novice priest that I was, treated me as a partner.

Many a time I remember reporting to him about something I had messed up and he very gently would tell me, "Well, I don't think I would have done it that way. Perhaps next time you might..." then he would suggest an alternative manner of handling the situation.

One of the greatest lessons I learned from him and other experienced priests like him was humility. After five to ten years of seminary training, prayer, and formation and at the prime age of 26 or 27, a newly ordained man is expected, and even believes at times, that he has all the answers!

"Father, I have a teenage son who won't go to church. What should I do about it?" Or, "Father, my wife is angry with me because she says I don't 'communicate'. What can I do?" Or, "Father, my little girl won't do her homework. Will you talk with her?"

It is as if the laying on of hands by the bishop gives a young priest insight into child rearing, marriage counseling, and the ability to leap tall buildings! I suspect the faithful see a young priest as an opportunity to get a fresh look and a new energy to old problems. But a young priest doesn't always see it that way. He sees it as his ordained responsibility to make a difference, to give pearls of wisdom, and to be involved in whatever problem is brought to him and to solve these problems!

My pastor wisely allowed me to accept many of these situations and calmly watched as I become more and more frustrated. Finally he said, "You can't carry everyone's burdens. All you are asked to do is to walk with them as they carry their own burdens. That in itself is enough."

It is a hard lesson to learn. Only after getting mixed up in the age old fight of school dress codes at a school council meeting (but I learned so much about high top tennis shoes!), or after putting myself in the middle of an Altar Society debate as to who should use the society's linen table cloths, and especially after involuntarily becoming a referee between a husband and wife's yelling match during a "marriage counseling" session, did I learn humility. The ability to realize: I don't have all the answers!

The one area I could make a difference was with the dying. I quickly learned this was a circumstance where only a priest can journey. Not being Simon of Cyrene is frustrating. You want to carry their pain, carry their cross. But the priesthood is often being Veronica instead, wiping away the blood and tears. Or being the Blessed Mother standing at the foot of the cross. Or Saint John, being faithful, and not running away.

Again, I remember the time of day. It was around 2pm. I had just finished a funeral of one parishioner whom I had walked with to eternity, and was informed of another who had just passed. Immediately I went to the home. He had just died.

After praying the prayers for the dead, I assisted his wife, now his widow, in smoothing the bed sheets, cleaning his face, and closing his eyes before the mortuary came for his body. He was a man of grace, so even in death we knew he would want to look his best.

He died as the result of a botched surgery. It was an unnecessary death. I tried, with limited success, to help him through the anger he felt. When finally he and his wife asked the question that always gets asked, I was prepared.

"Why did this happen?" They asked. Responding with the humility that I had come to know, I said, "I don't know." As I looked up, I saw the clock which read, "3pm." The hour of our Lord's death. I went on, "I don't know. But I know the Lord is with us!"

I don't need to have all the answers, but if I can point out His Presence, that is enough. An important lesson for a priest whose oils are still fresh from ordination.

"Have no fear of moving into the unknown. Simply step out fearlessly knowing that I am with you, therefore no harm can befall you; all is very, very well. Do this in complete faith and confidence."

-Pope John Paul II

Newly Ordained: Too Young?

You expect to show your driver's license to a police officer when pulled over for speeding or some other traffic infraction. You can expect to show your driver's license at the airport security. A driver's license shows who you are, when you were born, and where you live.

You don't expect to have to show your driver's license while trying to minister the Anointing of the Sick to a little old lady in a gown with a slit up the backside that keeps flapping open and is demanding proof that you are old enough to be a priest!

But that's what happened. Ahh, the perils of the newly ordained priest.

I was newly ordained and twenty seven years old. I received a call late in the evening. This was before pagers, let alone cell phones. (Yes, there was a time! I think they call it the "silent ages") the nurse on the phone wanted me to come immediately to the hospital to give a patient the "last rites."

Not wanting to ask if the patient really needed or wanted the Last Rites, which are Anointing of the Sick, Confession, and Holy Communion, I instead asked if the patient was actively dying giving me an indication as to what was happening.

"No," the nurse said, "she is pretty 'active,' but not dying. She is about to have a medical procedure to determine what is wrong and is demanding a priest." As if to accentuate her, I could hear commotion in the background.

"I'll be right there." I said. Contrary to popular myth, one which I believe we priests perpetuate, it is unusual to be called to come to the hospital. People are too kind, excusing us when we are yawning in the confessional before the 6:30am Mass.

"Oh Father is tired this morning. He must have been called out in the middle of the night. Poor man." We are not quick to correct and tell them it was really the re-run of *Star Trek: The Next Generation* that kept us up till the middle of the night. Our hospital chaplains do such a great job, that we parish priests normally can visit the sick within our normal scheduled day.

This time, however, the lady was a parishioner of my parish and wanted her parish priest to see her. As I entered the room where they were prepping her for the procedure, the before mentioned gown distracted me, and I cast my eyes anywhere but upon my parishioner and gown. When I finally did regain my composure, she was glaring at me.

"Who the devil are you?" She shrieked.

"I'm Father Ken." I told her.

"I don't know you!" She replied.

Seeing I wasn't getting anywhere, and ignoring the gown, I concentrated on her face, and explained that I was new to the parish, recently replacing the other associate pastor. After explaining where the other associate went, I thought we could get down to business. The nurses were already giving me the "You need to get going, so we can get going" stare.

In seeing me get my oils out she recoiled from me (gown and all) shouting, "You ain't going to touch me!"

"Great!' I thought, and by now the nurses were really looking at me, probably calling security.

"I need to anoint you. You know, the Anointing of the Sick." I explained.

"You're too young to be a priest. I'll bet you are one of the 'sin-a-nears".

Knowing she meant a seminarian, a young man studying to be a priest, I tried to assure her I was ordained and no longer a seminarian.

"Prove it!" she exclaimed. How in the world could I do that, I wondered. It's not like you get an "I'm a Priest Card" from the bishop after ordination.

"I'll bet you're not even old enough to be a priest!" she said. Remember the Prophet Jeremiah's argument to the Lord that he was too young to be a prophet; I was beginning to think maybe I was too young for this.

"If I showed you my driver's license, would that be proof enough?" I asked.

Shrugging, she said, "I guess so." Giving her my driver's license, she carefully examined it. With the medication and probably in need of glasses, I am not sure what she could see.

By this time however, the nurses were well past the point of patience and I knew my window of opportunity was closing. Getting out my oils, I began the prayers and quickly anointed her.

Out of resignation or just simply orneriness, she had the last word: "I don't know if you're old enough to be a priest, but at least you can drive a car, even though it's probably your daddy's car."

The last I saw her was being wheeled into another procedure room, gown and all.

Out in the parking lot, I said a prayer of thanksgiving and got into my car; my very first new car. Recently purchased from money given in part at ordination and Dad! Today I don't have the problem of having to prove I am a priest.

Older and hopefully wiser. But also thankful to our gracious God that we still have young men who look too young to be priests. Perhaps we should give them some sort of Priest ID. But no. Give them time, and they too will grow in stature, maturity, and looking the part. What a blessing: our church is alive and well with priests both young and old!

Lost and Found

I can't tell you why I first decided to become a diocesan priest. I remember it though. It was after a Catholic school Mass in the fourth grade in the early 1970's. Returning from church entering the classroom with a flush of excitement of what I experienced at Mass, I thought, "That's what I want to do!"

What "that" was, I did not realize that day. A wise Trappist Abbot said the reason a man enters the monastery to become a monk is not the same reason he remains. As soon as you figure out why you are here you must throw that understanding out and start anew.

This is characteristic of all vocations: a monk, a priest, a married person. The reasons why a couple enters marriage will not be the same reasons they remain married 20 years later. For some this is exciting, growing this way; for others it is disconcerting, not remaining unchanged through the years.

While our reasons for remaining in our vocation might change, there is a foundation upon which each vocation is built. Ultimately the roots are found in our Baptismal call to love God, neighbor and self. At different times this love will take different forms, but there should be a central thread securing it throughout time.

As a diocesan priest my life is built upon several themes such as: "Go therefore, and make disciples of all nations... (Matthew 28:19)" or "I am the good shepherd... (John 10:11)," but one central theme I find often in my priesthood is "Go rather to the lost sheep... (Matt 10:6)"

I do a lot of finding. Finding people to come to church; finding youth to get them active; finding what Bible study would be helpful to the parish; finding the right people to led the Bible study; and of course there is the Lost and Found!

Every parish church has one. It is a closet, box, or shelf; either labeled or a place that everyone knows, housing all the items parishioners bring to church and fail to take home with them. Have you ever taken a peek at it? Contained inside this treasure box are: cameras, car keys, house keys, coats, scarves, teething toys, and plastic rings. There are always rosaries, jewelry, prayer books, clothing, and umbrellas...lots of umbrellas!

How can people lose some of these things? It is not unusual to find shirts, socks, pants, and even undergarments. Perhaps they are imitating the example of Saint Francis of Assisi who took off all his clothing, dramatically stating he was giving up everything to follow Jesus. I think I would have noticed that though.

In thinking about what people leave behind, perhaps a church is a good place to "lose things!" Not keys, clothing, or umbrellas, but worries, fear, and sin. Often a "lost and found" box will have printed on it the line from Luke's Gospel of the Prodigal Son, "He was lost, and now has been found!" (Luke 15) Maybe I should put a "Lost and Found" sign over the confessional.

With the first excitement about the priesthood in the fourth grade, I never thought about sitting in a small space listening to people pour out their hearts, and giving them forgiveness and courage. That understanding of why I am a priest came later.

My first experiences of hearing confessions were difficult. The confessional was a box where the penitents' windows were on both sides of me, and I in the middle. I felt like I was rowing oars, opening and closing windows at my left and right, often for many hours. The space was so cramped that sometimes penitents, right and left, would begin confessing their sins at the same time, both thinking I was speaking to them. Simultaneous confessions!

I labored to understand my role in the confessional. Was I to give advice? Fresh out of the seminary I did not understand some of these sins, let alone know how to advise against them. Was I to simply listen and give absolution? But some really needed help. They were truly lost and desired to be found...by me! I felt like I was suddenly in a foreign country. I was as lost too!

Gradually I understood the words "you need not worry about what you will say..." (Luke 12:11) for when I quite trying so hard the words came. Perhaps they were from my morning meditation, or a book I was using for spiritual reading; whenever words were needed, they were there. Later I came to understand that it wasn't the words spoken but the compassion of my own sinful humanity and the strong voice of Jesus through the Church giving solace.

Now after 19 years of priesthood, I can see parallels between the parish's lost and found box and my role in the Confessional. Again, as soon as you think you got it figured out, you have to refigure it.

I was finishing up some paperwork from a baptism in my office on a Sunday afternoon, when I noticed a note. It said to call a man whose wife lost something at Mass that day. Not unusual.

I called. Telling him who I was, I asked what his wife lost.

"Her uppers." He said.

"Her what???" I replied not understanding.

"Her uppers...her false teeth." He said as naturally as he was saying 'Her umbrella.'

"But I am sorry to have bothered you Father," He went on, "She thought she lost her uppers, but I found them in my shirt pocket when we got home."

This was a first for me, but wisely after 19 years of priesthood I didn't question how her teeth got lost in his pocket, and simply wished him a good day and hung up!

I suppose I shouldn't be so hard on people losing things at church. It's not all that unusual I suppose. In fact it's even Biblical, for Mary and Joseph lost Jesus in the Temple!

Of Brides and Men

She was not happy with me. The young lady on the telephone that is. After explaining that a wedding takes place in a church building, a sacred place within a sacred ceremony, and strolling down the aisle with an eight month old "flower girl" in a red wagon would not be appropriate, she was not pleased.

Weddings. The waterloo of a parish priest.

The relationship between a bride and a parish priest is a relationship between two voices speaking different languages. The voice of the priest is often a language of efficiency, of theology, and of "Get er' Done." It is the voice of a celibate male.

The voice of a bride speaks a language of uniqueness, exceptionality, and passion. It is the voice of a woman in love.

Combined with these two different voices is a choir of other voices from bridesmaids, groomsmen, mothers, fathers, stepmothers and fathers, to professional wedding coordinators and bride magazines. It is only by the grace of God that anyone gets married on a Saturday afternoon in a Catholic church because left to its own; these voices are capable of starting a war.

Oftentimes parish priests voice their anguish about weddings. This is sad, because a wedding should be a happy event, a time when two people become one with one another and one with the Church. The role of the priest is to witness a man and woman becoming one as spouses and to create an oneness between the couple and the Church, but this can be challenging.

Perhaps it's the circumstances of the ceremony itself. There are so many expectations for that one hour of that one day! It all has to be perfect. The pressure is sometimes too much for everyone!

Weddings often vacillate between two extremes: from a ceremony that every detail and minute before, during and after the wedding is choreographed; to a wedding where the couple seems to have just shown up and is not sure if they are at the right church.

I have a theory. I wonder if it's the clothing that creates an adverse atmosphere at a wedding. The bride has exercised, dieted, and worked hard to be able to fit in a dress that she couldn't have worn even in high school; the groom and groomsmen are playing dress-up in somebody else's clothes they have rented; and the bridesmaids often look like plums or tightly wrapped Hershey kisses with legs. I wonder if it's not all too much.

At every wedding I thank God for the invention of *Post It Notes*! I have trouble with names under pressure. And a wedding is not a place to fool around with names!

Generally the couple has not been active in the parish because they are just finishing school or perhaps one or both are not attending regularly, or one is not Catholic. I meet with them 3-4 times over the course of 6 months to a year. They attend a number of other formation classes but not always with me. So I don't always know the couple well.

And then there are the actual names. Whatever happened to Sally, Susan, or Pat? Or Saint names such as Mary and Veronica. (Of course there is also Blessed Kateri Tekakwitha!) Now we have names like Arianna, Destry, or Venita. At least men's names are stable, except for some like Gareth!

And then there are the names that are similar: Kaylee and Kylie; Tyler and Taylor; Brendon and Brandon. As soon as you think you got it down, you question yourself and you have to look it up again!

Thank goodness for *Post It Notes*. Right there in the ritual book, I place their names so I don't make a mistake. We have all seen a priest or minister mispronounce a name at a funeral. Embarrassing but people seem to understand. Call the bride by her sister's name at a wedding and mayhem breaks out.

There is nothing worse than calling a bride by the wrong name. Well, I guess there is one thing worse. After a particular long Friday, I went to the church for a wedding rehearsal. I got the names of the bride and groom on the mark; I even did well with some of the attendants. But I made a crucial mistake in calling the 'Sister of the bride' the 'Mother of the Bride!' They looked similar, only 25 years apart...oh well, *Post It Notes* can't solve everything. That was a long ceremony although the mother kept smiling at me!

After all the formation classes are completed, Nuptial Mass plans made, and the guests are dressed and have arrived; the bride in her baptismal white garment stands at the entrance of the church. This is the moment.

Two men await her at the altar representing two different relationships: one with a human spouse, one with the Church. It all comes together in a chorus at that moment. It can make all the fuss worthwhile at that moment!

And the bride who wanted her 8 month old flower girl to be rolled down the aisle? Well, in spite of my first-rate theological clarification, they snuck a bright, fire engine red wagon into the back of the church while I was processing down the aisle and proceeded to place the 8 month old flower girl onto it for the procession.

My heart was pounding as I saw the flower girl being readied to be rolled down the aisle and I silently prayed to our Blessed Virgin for calm and acceptance, only to then see the child being whisked away in a flurry after having vomited all over the wagon and one of the bridesmaids.

Being twirled round and round by the 7 year old ring bearer prior to the procession did not seem to agree with her.

I suppressed a smile.

Waiting and Advent

The life of a parish priest can be compared with a fireman. We fluctuate between working furiously and waiting for the next event. In our modern world, we wait a lot: for the copier to warm up; for a teenager to quit "texting" and respond to a question; waiting on hold while the person who called you, takes another call! We all do a lot of waiting...and we don't like it!

The "waiting" a parish priest does is not unique: waiting for appointments, for a plane, for the next sports season. But a unique wait, known only to a priest, is waiting in the confessional.

A confessional is a one of a kind place. Some are like a broom closet, others so cozy and nice, you are tempted to stay. For those who do not go to Confession, it is a secretive mysterious place. For those who regularly go to Confession, it is a secure and calm place. For a parish priest, it is a bit of both.

I remember my first confessional. The priest would sit in a four by four foot "closet" with penitents on each side, in spaces not much bigger. Separating the priest from the penitent was a metal grill window with a sliding wood door.

"Bang!" I hear the penitent slam down on the wooden kneeler, wondering if they hurt themselves. The kneeler raised off its base slightly would lower onto a connection when a penitent knelt down. This connection caused the light outside the confessional to be red.

As I "slapped" the wooden sliding door reached the end of its destination inside the window, I would begin: "In the Name of the Father…" Like bells ringing on a church steeple, that "bang" and "slap" are fixed into my mind as sounds of devotion and reverence.

Most parishes have confessions prior to daily Mass, Saturday afternoons and evenings. Seminary professors told me in the 1980's that Catholics could no longer be found in Confessional lines Saturday afternoon's. I humbly have found this not to be the case.

During the Advent and Lenten seasons lines are long, but in the summer there are often intervals between groups of people. In these pauses the priest is left waiting and can choose to use this time in a number of ways: some good, or some not so good.

What can he do?

He can pray. The rosary is a great prayer while waiting. Often I use each bead to remember a particular person to intercede for or a particular gift I am thankful to the Lord. That's sixty prayers! People are always asking me to pray for them; this is a concrete way I can.

He can read the Scripture. Always keeping a Bible handy, I read next Sunday's Gospel, reflect on my homily, or just at random open the Bible to see where my finger will land and what the Lord might say to me in this passage. It's quite fun and amazing how the Lord speaks in this way. Rarely does my finger land on a list or genealogy.

He can use the time journaling, writing down thoughts for future homilies. It is amazing when I re-read my spiritual journals, how I get some difficulty understood, only to forget it next week. With a spiritual journal I see progress in my journey to God, and not forget a prior understanding.

He can read. The quiet allows for slow spiritual reading or Lectio Divina (Sacred Reading). Reading the lives of the Saints inspires me to think and act differently. Sacred reading is a slow, prayerful reading, where God's voice is heard. Waiting is perfect for sacred, prayerful reading.

He can also day dream, thinking of where he would rather be, or what he could be doing instead of waiting. He can replay past conversations or rehearse what he will say to a person who is difficult. Replay and rehearse!

He can use the time to worry, allowing voices in his head about finances, relationships, insecurities, or resentments to be heard. The Devil can be quite mocking when a person waits.

Or finally he can leave. After watching the time pass, he can decide if parishioners want to go to Confession they should be here earlier and he is too busy and his time too important to be waiting.

Surprised with all the options a priest has while waiting in the confessional? Advent is a time of waiting too: waiting for Christmas day with family; waiting for the break from school or work; and ultimately waiting to see Jesus face to face for our pilgrimage on earth is really just a period of waiting.

Waiting inside the confessional might be exclusive to priests, but waiting is not. Nor what we do while waiting.

The Advent season is a practice in waiting allowing us to try new things while waiting. Re-read what a priest can do in the confessional waiting to see if there are some ideas for your Advent. As a priest waiting in the confessional, the Advent waiting season can also be either a time of grace or a time of frustration.

One option that I failed to mention a priest can do is sleep. Occasionally I must admit my eyes droop and suddenly I hear the "bang" of the kneeler. Stuttering, trying to gain my composure, I am reminded of what our Lord said, "Be alert! You do not know when the time will come!" (Mark 13:33) Waiting. A time of grace...if we allow it.

"He loves, He hopes, He waits. If He came down on our altars on certain days only, some sinner, on being moved to repentance, might have to look for Him, and not finding Him, might have to wait. Our Lord prefers to wait Himself for the sinner for years rather than keep him waiting one instant."

Saint Peter Julian Eymard

Catholic Enough?

I could not tell if they really wanted me there or not, but I went anyway. As a parish priest, I receive various opportunities and requests asking for my ministry and presence and most of the time I am very welcomed as an ambassador of Christ, but occasionally I am not.

Walking in a public place can often be a gauntlet. I remember the time walking through the halls of the hospital and being recognized by some former parishioners. After the initial greeting and small talk they asked, "Father, would you come and see my father in law?" Of course, they always catch you as you are leaving the hospital. "Yes, where is he?" I respond. Of course again, it is always the furthest part of the hospital that you just came from.

When a priest walks into a hospital room, he has to render an immediate assessment: Am I wanted? How long do they want me to stay? Are they parishioners? Am I talking to the right patient? Are they "practicing Catholics?"

As I enter the room with the family, I am greeted by Bob Barker of The Price is Right game show on television. (You might make a note: Never go to a nursing home during The Price is Right...even without Bob Barker!) Between the thunderous television and the numerous people in the room, I was trying to get a feel whether the patient was Catholic, desired the Sacrament of the Sick and Holy Communion. I was also trying to decide how to get the television off in case he wanted me to hear his confession. (Many a Confession has been heard during The Price is Right! Maybe we could use some of that technology in the Confessional? 'Win a brand new car when you go to Confession if you guess your penance!)

This time my assessments were unnecessary.... "Hey, who are you?" the patient yelled out, "are you the undertaker? I'm not dead yet! Get the _____ out of here."

Explaining I was a Catholic priest didn't seem to lift up his disposition in the least. I got the impression Catholic priests were just one level up from being an undertaker, and far below Bob Barker! I quietly slipped out.

Today, the request came from a mortuary. Not unusual. I have found morticians can be of great service for the Lord and the Church, guiding a family to receive needed spiritual help. A family had experienced the sudden death of a child due to an accident in the home. I couldn't tell if the family was requesting me or if the mortician felt overwhelmed and called me. I went anyway.

The drive between the parish and mortuary is a short one, but many thoughts and prayers goes through my head: What am I walking into? Who are they? Do they attend regularly? What do they want me to do?

Between praying and worrying, I arrived. Their eyes light up when I entered the small room crammed with family. I quickly assessed I did not know the family, nor did they know me. They were past the initial shock and were now trying to make sense of all the funeral arrangements. Less than five hours ago they were deciding what breakfast cereal to pour into the bowl. Now they had to decide between wood and metal caskets for their child. It was all too much.

We first prayed to Our Mother of Sorrows. By praying with a family, I get a feel where they are spiritually. Beginning the Sign of the Cross, I glanced around to see if other hands in the room were also making the Sign of the Cross. Sure enough, they were Catholic, praying along with me through the intercession of Our Lady.

Afterwards, they introduced themselves and said they did not come to church very often. "In fact," the mother said, "we only go at Christmastime. We ought to do better but..." I assured her in due time she would begin coming to Church, but right now the Church would come to them.

Finishing the funeral arrangements, we began to talk about their child: who she was, why her life mattered, what happened. They wanted me to know all about her. And I was glad to listen.

The usual questions surfaced: Why did God do this? Was it because they weren't "practicing Catholics?" Why did this happen? I had no answers for them. I could only be present as they poured out the many conflicting emotions of grief, anger, and love.

The funeral went well. The family spoke of how the music, the ritual, and the atmosphere of the sacredness of the church brought them solace in burying their child.... and I haven't seen them since.

We invited them to a yearly memorial Mass, but they did not come. The parish sent a Mass card a few months later, but no response. Perhaps someday after a Christmas Mass, one of the family members will come up to me and say, "Remember me? You were there for my family when my sister died!" Sometimes this happens, often it does not.

Maybe I should have asked the mortician if the family were "practicing Catholics" and registered in my parish before I came to visit them, or required church attendance more than Christmas or Easter before the resources of the parish provided for a funeral. I suppose if I felt that way, I would need to start my own church because that is neither the Catholic Church nor the priesthood of the Church.

No, the family was truly Catholic. They may not regularly attend Sunday Mass right now or fill out their stewardship forms for time, talent, or treasure, but my assessment of them was on the mark: they are Catholic through and through because they recognized in a time of grave need, their need for the Church. And they recognized me, a priest of the Church, as an ambassador of Christ. And that is Catholic enough for me!

"Charity is certainly greater than any rule. Moreover, all rules must lead to charity."
-St. Vincent de Paul

Rock Star Status

The air was bitter cold and the boy's head was covered with a stocking cap pulled over his ears. I saw him before out the rectory window, playing on the playground. Now I was out walking my dog and the boy was leaving on his bicycle. His grandmother and little sister followed.

I get many smiles and even honking of horns walking the neighborhood with my dog. Perhaps it is the black clothes contrasted by the white dog. Or the unexpected sight of a man, praying a rosary, while a little white dog is happily following. This time the attention was more subtle.

The little boy, obviously a novice cyclist, was very intent on watching where he was going when he looked up. Seeing me, recognition flashed across his eyes and a smile that would brighten the coldest day. I said "Hello," not wanting to wave at him fearing he would lift a hand to wave back only to crash the bike into the curb spilling him.

After the entourage of Grandmother and little sister went by, I heard the boy say to his grandmother, "That person" pointing my direction with great emphasis, "He's a priest!" Words that can melt the heart of a priest!

Many years ago, I heard other words: "Are you resolved to consecrate your life to God for the salvation of his people, and to unite yourself more closely every day to Christ the High Priest, who offered himself for us to the Father as a perfect sacrifice?" The Bishop asked us.

"I am, with the help of God!" I and the two other young men responded at my ordination into the priesthood. The Bishop had already asked three other questions, of which we responded, "I am," but this was the final question, summing up the rest, therefore requiring an additional understanding I could not do this without the help of God.

Actually it was with the help of the Master of Ceremonies, who through a pre-arranged signal of placing his hand over his heart, we knew to add the "with the help of God."

The Master of Ceremonies is that priest often garbed in a cassock and surplice allowing the ceremonies with the bishop to run smooth. The "MC" as they are called, makes everyone, especially the bishop, look good and yet is unseen. Don't you wish you had a MC at your workplace?

In some ways, I was so worried about missing the hand signal and not responding correctly, I am not sure if I really heard the words the bishop was saying. Oh, I knew the words because I had studied them, prayed over them, and reflected upon them with my spiritual director for many months before.

Like many moments in the ordination rite, it wouldn't be until after I had entered into the sacrament I would understand what the words meant. I understood then, I could not successfully consecrate my life to God without God's help, but today I would add a number of other God-given helps too.

One of those helps is the children. Every priest will testify when having a bad day, all it takes is a visit to the school cafeteria, the hallways, or classroom. The Cafeteria ladies dread my visits so excited do the children become. I've learned to stand in the doorway and wave. Nothing will lift your spirits like having a hundred or so children wave excitedly at you.

Children also know what the priesthood is all about. Probably twice a month, sometimes more often, a parent will pull me aside and say, "You won't believe what little Johnny said about you!"

Actually, by that time, I know what is coming next. They continue, "You walked by at Mass and little Johnny said, 'Look there's Jesus!' Isn't that cute!?!" The parent proudly says. "Yes," I generally respond to them although they rarely hear me, so caught up in what they saw as adorable.

"Yes, little Johnny truly understands the sacrament character of Holy Orders. I am *in persona Christi,* in the person of Christ. A priest, who is a sharer, as St. Thomas wrote, in the priesthood of Christ, offers the Mass in the Person of Christ."

Such notoriety could give me a Rock Star Status, but in fact is very humbling to know Jesus chose me to carry out publically the priestly ministry in His name and on behalf of mankind. That being said, I still relish the attention as did our Lord when he welcomed the little children (Mt. 19:14). You would be a fool not to recognize the encouragement and reminder God is giving you through a child. This can be easily forgotten unless one remembers 'ad majorem dei gloriam', all for the glory of God!

Lions and Lambs, Oh My!

Generalizations are dangerous but if you were to separate parish pastors by style it would be lambs and lions. A lamb is the gentle, compassionate pastor who sees each person as an individual, and deals with situations case by case, person by person knowing each situation can be different. A lamb is sacrificial of their time and lives.

The lion is the bold pastor with the ability of making tough decisions, seeing the bigger picture, dealing with situations with equality and justice knowing how you respond to one parishioner is how you respond consistently with all. A lion will stand up for what needs to be done and robustly lead people to new heights.

Neither is right or wrong. Both have advantages and disadvantages. The disadvantage of a lamb is indecisiveness, getting stuck in details, and being seen as having favorites; the lion can be seen as distant, reserved, and uncaring to the individual, concerned only with the overall organization.

If you want selflessness, sacrifice, and devotion ask a lamb. If you want boldness, courage and efficiency ask a lion. Both are necessary in the life of the Church and every priest has a bit of both, but generally one or the other dominates. In smaller parishes, the pastor knows people quickly and intimately; a pastor's lamb-side shepherds. In large parishes where he is literally serving the masses of people, the lion roars. I can be both but my naturally tendency is to be a lion...with saber teeth!

After a particular hard day because my lion came out of the cave taking no prisoners, I was walking back to the rectory. Meeting with a family, I insisted upon making no exceptions to a particular rule ("If you do it for one, you must do it for all" the Lion said). I returned to the rectory a different route than normal. I didn't want to tempt my fuming parishioners into sin by presenting myself as a target on the road! Actually I knew I was safe, but needed the longer route to process what happened and try to answer the question of: "Is this why I became a priest? I must be doing it wrong!"

Once home my emergency pager sounded. A parishioner's father was dying. Still disturbed by the earlier meeting, I slowly prayed the Serenity Prayer. Usually after a "Lion meets Bambi" meeting I am more concerned about *how* I acted, than *what* I decided.

Arriving at the house, I could see the street was a parking lot. The family has been called and was gathering. Entering the house I received a few nods of acknowledgement but also some shakes of the head. There was even a "Who called him?" behind me. I was called by the man's daughter who regularly attended Mass at the parish. She was very faith filled and because of her zeal, I imagine might be a source of conflict for those who did not attend church regularly.

As a lion I confidently entered the bedroom, knelt down beside the bed, introduced myself and quickly got to the business at hand: "Would you like to pray? Let's also go to Confession!"

His eyes widened with recognition of who I was and nodding his head gave consent to God's mercy. Feeling like Jesus in Mark 5:40, I asked for everyone to leave. One of the sons with a scowl on his face was hesitant to leave his father alone with me, but knowing I had only a small window of opportunity to hear the Confession, I firmly said, "I only need a few minutes alone with your Dad, right now."

Leaving he spoke, "Dad, I'll be right outside the door!" I am sure he would have bust the door down if he heard any cry of distress from his father while I was with him. I understood his anguish and also knew his father needed me. Thankfully the confession was short yet sincere. Ushering the family back into the room, we celebrated the final two sacraments: Anointing of the Sick and Holy Communion (Viaticum). These three sacraments, Confession, Anointing, and Communion comprise the "last rites."

Before giving him Holy Communion, I gently spoke with the family how their father was now to embark in the greatest adventure of his life. How he had lived an entire lifetime to come to this point of meeting our God face to face and to be embraced by Love itself. How he would be experiencing our God, all the while we would experience sadness. They seemed to take comfort in these words.

After reading from John's Gospel of how the Father's house has many rooms and Jesus would prepare a place for us (John 14), I left the house. Out in my car I offered a prayer for the dying man and his family, but most of all for allowing me this experience of realizing why I was a priest.

With all the mixed emotions I felt after meeting with the school family, this experience made me realize God uses my weakness as strength. With my entire lioness, I was able to walk into an awkward and possibly challenging situation bringing the presence of Christ. Kneeling before the family, my words and presence was that of the Lamb of God. (See 2 Co 12: 9-10)

Yes, pastors can be seen as either a lion or a lamb. We need both in the church. Like Our Father's House which has many rooms, so He has provided us with many different pastors. Pray for your pastors so they can be whatever the parish or situation may need at the given moment: "all things to all people" bringing us to Christ. (See 1 Corinthians 9)

"To convert somebody go and take them by the hand and guide them."
-St. Thomas Aquinas

A Priest can change too!

I think I shocked them. It gets me into trouble though, but I still do it. I like to think I am following the Lord who also seemed to like to shock people ("If your eye is causing you to sin, pluck it out!" Mt 5:29-30, "You should hate your mother and father..." Luke 14:26). They are called hyperboles. Exaggerations to make a point, e.g., "I've been there a million times!" Sometimes I wonder if I don't do it just because I am a bit ornery.

The young couple was being prepared by me for the Sacrament of Marriage. While I've never been married, I do know something about perseverance. Their eyes were opened wide and mouths slightly opened. I had just told them, "If I had known everything I would face as a priest, I wouldn't become a priest!" The point I hoped to make was the future is filled with both joy and sorrow. Knowing future hardships can paralyze us, so we step forward in faith. God doesn't reveal to us everything that we will be faced with, but will change us to be able to face anything.

If I knew all I would be faced with, I would be overwhelmed. I could not do then, what I can do now. I am not the same person as I was then...thank goodness. The Lord continues to change me.

We all expect to change, but sometimes it is surprising to see a priest change. I remember in my home parish after my pastor attended a priestly renewal conference, he came back full of life, remorse of past sins, and you could see he changed.

Another priest I knew was quite adamant the Blessed Virgin Mary could not be appearing at a particular place. After his journey there, against his better judgment, he came back very changed.

It is humbling for us priests to accept change in ourselves when we spend so much of our time advocating change and conversion in our parishioners. I experienced this first hand when I became a pastor. My associate was from Vietnam. He, newly ordained, was on fire with the Lord and for the people. I on the other hand, was a seasoned pastor of at least 2 years! (Ahh, how naïve I was!)

My associate wanted to celebrate the sacrament of Baptism for Vietnamese parishioners separately from the English speaking parishioners. Knowing they understood English and not wanting to create divisions in a sacrament that is to unite, I did not want him to celebrate separate liturgies.

Coming through the Church one Sunday afternoon, I was surprised to see a gathering of people around the baptismal font. There amidst a group of Vietnamese parishioners, was my associate...baptizing a baby. With great indignation I strode forward to demand what was going on, but was stopped by the gorgeous melody being chanted. Back and forth, family, priest and parishioners were praying in Vietnamese to the glories of God.

Not visible, I continued to listen and marvel at the devotion and prayerful atmosphere I saw. After the ceremony, as my associate was putting things away, I stepped forward. He was surprised to say the least! My righteous anger by this time had turned to admiration.

No, he should not have done something I asked him not to do, but I admired him nonetheless, and told him so. "What a beautiful ceremony!" I said. He sheepishly explained the prayer rhythm in which Vietnamese Catholics pray and why it was so important to continue their Catholic culture in America. I whole heartedly agreed!

After a heart to heart discussion, I learned in his culture you don't question authority. What the person in authority says is not to be questioned. I explained how in our culture, such questions are expected and even encouraged so the leader can learn and make necessary changes. We got along smoothly from then on.

Change is conversion, in Latin conversio, a turning around. I am not the same priest I was at ordination. Why I became a priest is not the same reasons I remain a priest. Like spouses, my relationship with the church has grown and changed over the years.

Recently I've taken another 'turn around.' When newly ordained I noticed older priests celebrating the Mass slowly. That irritated me. Didn't they understand people have families, are busy, and anything longer than 50 minutes for Sunday Mass or 20 minutes for daily Mass is too long.

With one eye on the Missal and the other on the clock, I learned to celebrate the Mass in efficient fashion. I would relish in the compliment, "Father got us out in less than 50 minutes!" What I heard them say is: "Father understands. We like Father!"

After years of hearing Confessions, I realized people do not pray. The most they are praying is at Sunday or daily Mass. I 'turned around' my thinking after realizing I was leading them in the most important hour of their entire week. I began to slow down, praying the First Eucharistic prayer (the long one) more, lingering longer in the prescribed silences, leading my people and self into a deeper prayer.

This conversion surprised me. I also found that people didn't complain, and they still left in a timely manner, filled with prayer.

Even priests need conversion. And that's no exaggeration!

"Late have I loved you, O Beauty ever ancient, ever new, late have I loved you!"
-St. Augustine

Just a little faith

It had been a long process and the past few weeks took their toll on me. He was a good man with young adult children and a wife. He was not ready to go home to the Lord, but the Lord nonetheless called him home on an early June morning. He wanted to see the birth of his second grandchild; the Lord only graced him with seeing the first.

I did my best to prepare him to be embraced by the Lord. We celebrated all the sacraments, prayed, spoke of the scripture passages about the kingdom of heaven (Matthew 6 & 25; John 14; Luke 16 & 20). The family called me about 1:30 in the morning telling me he was gone. I had left him about 10pm the night before at the hospice unit knowing it would be soon, but still the call surprised me. I did not go back to sleep easily.

Immediately I begin to think: "Was he prepared?" "What more could I have done?" Then deeper thoughts: "I wonder what he is experiencing right now. I wonder if what all I said, prayed, read with him is true… What if I am wrong?" In the darkness of the night, the devil uses doubt like a pickaxe. Methodically picking away at the mountain called faith.

The funeral was prayerful. The family peaceful knowing the pain and struggle was over, but a lingering, persistent doubt found its way into my daily prayer. The mountain was not crumbling, but fissures were formed.

A most powerful moment as a priest is to prepare others to go home to the Lord. It is the purpose of our life: to know Him, to love Him, and to serve Him in this world and to be happy with Him forever in the next life. I see the sick and dying as a priority and been with many in this process. If I did not believe in eternal life, than all was useless.

Why this man's death caused me to pause, I don't know, but I am thankful. Socrates said, "An unexamined life is not worth living." The same can be said of our faith life. To grow in faith, we must experience dark nights.

The phone rang again. This time it was about 11:30pm, awakening me from a deep sleep. The voice was of a man, who obviously had been drinking.

"Will I go to Hell if I kill myself?" the voice asked in a drunken accent.

What a theological quandary. Do I explain the necessity of deliberate consent in committing a mortal sin? How alcohol would most likely prevent him from such consent? Or how suicide is often the result of a mental illness or grave emotional trauma rendering a person not culpable for their actions. By doing so, will he then commit the grievous act?

Or do I tell him, 'Yes, you will go to hell, so don't do it?' Although the result might be saving his life, the ends never justify the means.

In such situations I've learned not to answer the question. Instead I got him to talk. He explained he was a Catholic from Korea and came to the area for work a couple of years ago.

His family was still in Korea. At first the conversation was fruitful, but after twenty minutes he began to cycle, saying the same things over and over. He was drinking as we spoke and not having a clue as to what he was saying. "Telephonitis" they call it. Finally becoming angry towards me, the church, God, and apple pie, he became vulgar.

I had enough. I told him I would be happy to see him tomorrow, but right now he needed some sleep (and so did I). His tirade began anew. Finally I said, "Listen, I'm hanging up. Call me in the morning!" And I hung up.

Heart pounding, eyes wide open, I laid there...for a long time. Playing, replaying, and again replaying what happened. Wondering if the police were in route to where he was because neighbors heard a gunshot. I would be responsible! Why did I hang up? Why wasn't I more patient? A better priest could have handled it better.

Finally, exhausted, I decided to pray. Very specifically asking the man who just died to intercede on the behalf of this man and to keep him safe. A peace came over me but I slept fitfully. Awaking the next morning, I was anxious and worried, wondering what happened to my late night caller. Did he kill himself? How can I find out???

Her name was Joan. She made an 11am appointment with me two weeks before. I did not know her or why she was coming to see me. She wanted to see a priest. As she sat down she explained her desire to accept God back into her life. She was a fallen away Catholic but attending an alcohol outpatient rehab program and her counselor suggested her return to church.

Although she had been sober for several months, she realized relapses were very probable. She shared her surprise how the rehab was celebrating graduation of five clients this very morning before she came, and one client, a Korean man was to graduate today but showed up hung over and would be going through the rehab again.

I sat back in my chair, closed my eyes, and thanked God that the man was safe and for the power of intercessory prayer of those with faith. Imagine that! All it takes is a little faith, and mountains get moved!

"We always find that those who walked closest to Christ were those who had to bear the greatest trials."
-St. Teresa of Avila

What they did <u>not</u> teach in the Seminary

While in the seminary, there were two sayings heard from every returning alumni priest. The first: "Enjoy it while it lasts!" I hated that saying! It implied the hardships of the seminary formation were nothing compared to what the hardships of priesthood were. Great! Something to look forward too!

The other was the other extreme: "My best day in the seminary is not better than my worst day in the priesthood." Rather embellished I believe. There were some very outstanding days in the seminary, and some pretty awful days in the priesthood. I think we are comparing apples to oranges.

That is the danger of seminary formation or any formation: marriage preparation, job training, or boot camp for the military. Preparation is not the real thing.

There are many things "they" did not teach me in the seminary, for example, when you have confessions from 7-8pm, why people all arrive at 7:55pm. Or why the same persons, no matter what day it is, rain or shine, are always late for Mass. Or how to tell the mother of the groom, "No, I won't tell your son not to marry *'that'* girl." These things you learn from experience to simply accept them, or try.

One thing not taught is how parishioners would receive Holy Communion. As Catholics we receive either on the tongue or in the hand, but people have adopted very odd ways of receiving.

In describing these "practices," I in no way wish to be sacrilegious, but perhaps in sharing the view of the Communion line from the eyes of a priest, it might assist reception in a more worthy manner. Habits change into character and there is no more important habit than to receive our Lord at Holy Communion.

From the Communion line I see:

The Lunger. This is the person who at the very last moment lunges at me, mouth agape, nearly engulfing my hand. At the very least, I get licked, at the worst, gummed.

The Snapping Turtle. Also known as a "biter." This person who instead of protruding their tongue to receive, will bite at the Host, often including the tips of my fingers.

The Licker. Similar to the Lunger, this person always gets my hand with their tongue no matter how hard I try.

The Bird. They tilt their head back as if at the dentist or like a bird receiving nourishment. Difficult especially if they are tall.

The Snake. This person does not open their mouth to receive, but rather protrudes their tongue in lightning fashion in and out, like a snake.

The Grabber. They receive by hand, but instead of receiving on his or her palm, will make the attempt to grab the Host.

The Clueless. This person creates a quandary for me. They extend their hands and protrude their tongue. When presented such a choice, I always distribute to the tongue.

The Boat. Receives by hand, but they extend both hands, not flat, but curved toward one another like the hull of a boat or a bowl. Either hand you place the host, it could be dropped.

The One Hander. Often this person is holding a baby or squirmy child in their arms, they come forward with child in one hand and extending the other hand, expecting to receive Holy Communion and then palm it into their mouth, trying to navigate past the child who often will try to grab. When holding a child, it is best to receive on the tongue.

The Two Hander. This person receives by hand, but when they come forward, both hands are extended far apart. Now I have to guess which one.

The Deer in the Headlights. Coming forward, they make no response looking startled as if they were passing by; saw a line, got into it just to see where everyone is going. As a priest, I've learned to delicately ask, "Are you a Catholic?" If yes, then I distribute; if no, I offer a blessing. Often they are non-Catholic and are appreciative of the blessing.

I debated in sharing the view I see at the Communion line because I did not want to make light of the enormous graces given at that moment, but because of these graces I thought I should share what a priest experiences at this sacred moment. It can be frustrating! I must not be alone for Saint Cyril of Jerusalem (315-386) felt compelled to address the same issue in the Fourth Century when he wrote:

> *"When you approach, take care not to do so with your hand stretched out and your fingers open or apart, but rather place your left hand as a throne beneath your right, as befits one who is about to receive the King. Then receive him, taking care that nothing is lost."*

Here is a reminder: Receive Holy Communion in the state of grace. If properly disposed, then receive either on the tongue or by hand. If you are receiving it on the tongue, tilt your head back slightly and extend your tongue far enough so there is no danger of the Host falling. If you receive in your hand, place one hand on top of the other, palms up, and receive the Host with one hand and place it in your mouth with the other.

The reception of Holy Communion is a true act of Faith that requires knowledge and reverence allowing us to receive God's free gift of grace. No, they did not teach us everything in the Seminary.

Who is the Greatest?

Three things take a parish priest by surprise: the inability of otherwise intelligent parishioners to spell the word "altar" (generally they spell it "alter"); the uncanny ability of some parishioners to know how you spend your free time causing you to wonder if they are following you; and lastly the naming of a brother priest as a bishop.

In the seminary, every young man aspires naively to become a bishop. As a parish priest you realize what a distant and difficult post being a bishop is. A bishop has the authority to ordain men, offer the Sacrament of Confirmation, dedicate churches and altars; he is a successor of the Apostles! They exercise the fullness of the priesthood, so the more a priest falls in love with the priesthood, the more he would embrace its fullness seen in the office of bishop.

After a diocesan brother was named a bishop I shared my conflicting emotions of sadness, joy, and traces of envy to a parishioner. He was surprised at my reaction. "I don't think people would realize priests would feel that way." he said. After our conversation I went to the gospel for reflection and found: "Jesus turned to the Apostles and asked, 'What were you arguing about on the way?' But they remained silent. They had been discussing among themselves on the way who was the greatest." (Mark 9:33-34)

This egotistical episode of the Apostles is recorded by all three of the Synoptic Gospel writers (Matthew, Mark, Luke). Funny how such an embarrassing episode might have been left out, instead was included recording how human, and male, the apostles were.

The gospel passage sums up the three "cancers" a priest must deal with: comparing, competition, and complaining. A priest must wrestle with these cancers not within the parish, but within himself!

These three c's: comparing, competition, and complaining are an excellent foundation of an examination of conscience and especially when a priest is at the annual clergy conference. They are part of being human and some are surprised to find them in their parish priest. It makes us all too human.

Perhaps the origins of our comparing began when we measured our height as children and compared how tall we were against our brothers, sisters or parents. In the priesthood we compare our stature to the past pastor, to the success of the neighboring parish mission, or how well our finances are compared to last year.

Saint Paul dealt with comparing when he wrote, "I have been foolish. You compelled me, for I ought to have been commended by you. For I am in no way inferior to these "super apostles" even though I am nothing." (2 Corinthians 12 11)

So common is competition in society that recently the news reported parents were training nursing babies for sports in the hopes of giving the child an edge in future athletic competition. Seminary is a training ground for priests. A priest once said, "You will never be as holy as in the seminary." I was scandalized by the remark. Now I understand. In the seminary we were on the practice field; on the sidelines just aching to get into the game. We were anticipating joining the team with no aspirations for anything else but to work for the Lord.

Once on the playing field, our male "competition gene" turns on, and suddenly we were comparing ourselves to other priests, coming up short, and feeling compelled to compete. It wasn't enough to compete against the Devil, now we competed against one another. An obvious tactic of the Devil! We had taken St. Paul's words "Run so as to win!" (1 Corinthians 9:24) and ran toward the wrong prize!

And then there is the complaining. If you read about the Hebrews leaving Egypt (Book of Exodus) they had two constant complaints: the location lacking food (desert) and the decisions of the leader (Moses). This can be summed up by "Where are we?" and "Who got us here?" For priests it can be summed up by: my assignment and the bishop!

Surprised priests' struggle with these things? Surprised we are so human? So male? It is our humanity, our struggles which allow us to rely upon God's grace for growth and holiness. We can't do it alone. It is in struggling with these normal human cancers that renders a priest valuable in the Confessional giving spiritual advice because we too struggle to cooperate with God's grace.

Recently I had a young man state he was not worthy to be a priest because of his weaknesses and wondered if he should quit thinking of the priesthood. I suggested it was because of his unworthiness that he would make an excellent priest.

When we are unworthy, we become dependent upon God alone.

My friends who have accepted the fullness of the Sacrament of Holy Orders as bishops have experienced this first hand too. They too consider themselves unworthy. It is by cooperating with God's grace they will become excellent bishops. After the conflicting emotions of surprise, joy, envy, and grief, it was sadness my heart settled upon: the sadness in letting go of a brother priest to become the apostle for another diocese.

I am reminded once more of Saint Paul writing to his brother priest Timothy: "I am grateful to God…as I remember you constantly in my prayers, night and day." (2 Timothy 1:3). It is these brothers who have become modern day apostles who give meaning to the words I pray at Mass: "Strengthen in faith and love your pilgrim Church on earth; your servant Pope Benedict, our Bishop, and all the bishops…"

With gratitude for both weaknesses and grace I embrace the priesthood, "for I can do all things in Christ who strengthens me." (Phil. 4:13)

"Let us go forward in peace, our eyes upon heaven, the only one goal of our labors."

St. Therese of Lisieux

Fathers

As priests, we are called "Father." For most priests, it was our earthy fathers who taught us to be spiritual fathers, for our earthly father introduced us to our Heavenly Father.

The greatest gift my mother and father gave me was my relationship with our Father in heaven. This gift is symbolized for me by a chair of all things! As a priest I have the privilege of sitting at the Presider's chair at church. The Presider's chair signifies the office of the priest in directing prayer "in persona Christi. " Before I was able to lead others to our loving Father from a Presider's chair, I first had to be led myself to another chair by my earthly father.

As a young boy, I shared a room with my older brother in the basement of our house. Basements can be shadowy, creepy places for a young boy with all the "creaks" a house makes as it settles or expands due to the temperature or having someone walk overhead.

Normally all these noises did not bother me because my older brother was with me. Even though I was a master at pestering him, following him, and generally annoying him, I knew he would protect me from anything lurking in the shadows of the dark basement bedroom that we shared. (I figured they would get him first, giving me time to escape!) But for a week or two, he was gone to scout camp, leaving me behind amongst the creatures lurking in the basement.

It was my father who first noticed that I wouldn't go to bed. It was unusual for me not to go to bed at bedtime, because I would normally read a Hardy Boy's book under the covers with a flashlight. When finally I did go to bed, I couldn't sleep with all the noises and shadows. My father, looking in on me, realized something was amiss, and sat on the edge of my bed.

He didn't laugh when I explained to him about the creatures in the shadows, or my fear of the ceiling caving in with all the popping noises of the floor above me as people walked on the floor above. Instead he simply went into the adjacent sewing room and got a chair and placed it at the foot of my bed.

Explaining how I did not need to be afraid of the noises or shadows, he said fear isn't always rational. "Sometimes we are afraid of things that just don't make any sense;" he said.

"What's the chair for?" I asked. "The chair is for Jesus. He loves you. He will protect you. And all you have to do when you are afraid is to ask him to sit at the foot of your bed to watch over you. He'll watch over you now."

It is through these simple acts, faith is passed from generation to generation. I asked my father where he came up with the idea of the chair before Parkinson's disease robbed him of the ability to speak: he said he didn't know. My mother said Dad read it in a devotional book but for him to remember and to share this story, I suspect it was from a simple life of prayer and recognizing Jesus in the different chairs of his life.

What a wonderful gift this is! Fatherhood! Giving your children the eyesight to see and recognize God!

Much of this article I stole from my recent homily at my father's funeral. As spiritual fathers, we are allowed to recycle good insights! While walking with my earthly father to his eternal home, I read the autobiography of Pope Benedict, "Milestones." When speaking of the death of his father, Pope Benedict wrote: "I sensed that the world was emptier for me and that a portion of my home had been transferred to the other world."

This is what fatherhood is about: creating a home in which we can see God. I sometimes wonder if young parents understand how the little things they say or do will remain with their child. I doubt if my father thought much of the chair incident, but after 40 some odd years, it remains with me.

Other impressions my father left me with was eating his toast over the sink while praying from his novena prayer book, or the family rosary in the car (a station wagon no less!). Every time I pray the rosary in the car now, I think of him. Small actions yielding great harvests! It is what my spiritual fatherhood is about and every Christian parents vocation.

I am very grateful for the gift my father has left me: the ability to experience God's presence here on earth, and the opportunity to see God face to face in heaven, for which you and I were created. And I look forward with hope to the day when I will meet my Heavenly Father face to face with my earthly father at His side.

Every year a diocesan priest is to take a canonical retreat. The Code of Canon Law states (Can. 276),

"In leading their lives, clerics are bound in a special way to pursue holiness since, having been consecrated to God by a new title in the reception of orders, they are dispensers of the mysteries of God in the service of His people.

In order to pursue this perfection: they are first of all to fulfill faithfully and tirelessly the duties of the pastoral ministry; they are to nourish their spiritual life from the two fold table of sacred scripture and the Eucharist; therefore , priests are earnestly invited to offer the Eucharist daily...priests are obliged to carry out the liturgy of the hours daily...they are equally bound to make time for spiritual retreats....they are urged to engage in mental prayer regularly, to approach the sacrament of penance frequently, to honor the Virgin Mother of God with particular veneration, and to use other common and particular means of sanctification."

Here is my report of one such retreat.....

Report from Retreat Number One: A nod speaks volumes.

I just stole a blanket. The seventh commandment is pretty explicit: Thy shall not steal. The catechism forbids unjustly taking or keeping the goods of one's neighbor. Further it states, "For the common good, it requires respect for the universal destination of goods and respect for the right to private property."

Yet, I am still with a blanket that is not mine. A pink one! Perhaps I should explain.

The "view from the rectory window" is of Chicago, Illinois, on a fall day. Mundelein, Illinois, to be specific at Saint Mary of the Lake Seminary. Surrounded by remarkable buildings and autumn changing trees reflecting on the lake, it has a colorful history.

Archbishop George Mundelein opened this seminary in 1921, the roaring 20's. The climate of the United States at the time was of suspicion towards Catholics whether we were true Americans. Conscious of this, Archbishop Mundelein hired a young Catholic architect, Joseph McCarthy and had him design all the buildings in the American neo-classical style to symbolize that the Catholic Church in America had come to age.

Mundelein even went so far as to model the main chapel after the First Congregational Church of Old Lyme, Connecticut and the Cardinal's Villa is a copy of George

Washington's Mount Vernon. In 1926 the International Eucharistic Congress was held here making transportation history by creating the largest movement of people by rail in the history of the country.

So, where does the pink blanket fit in? It is in this gorgeous setting, amidst the buildings set to establish Catholicity in America that 80 priests throughout the United States are together for an 8 day silent retreat.

What I wish to point out from the following sentence is: 80 MEN, 8 DAYS, and SILENT! Can you imagine what this looks like? Eighty men going and coming from chapel, to the chow hall, sitting at table eating, to and from conferences, with the only communication between them, a nod of the head!

For some, it was Hell. For others, such as me, wonder why we can't always live this way! "Hello's" and "How are you?" are vastly over used in our society, and I wonder if we wouldn't be better with just a nod of acknowledgement.

A nod of the head says: "Hi, I realize you exist. You are important, but listening to our Lord is more important right now. We can talk later...if we have too." I'll bet you had no idea a nod of the head meant so much!

Think about how our world would be different if talked less, listened to God more, and simply went about the business of living, rather than talking about living. Nations might acknowledge one another easier if they only had to nod at each other. Families might get along with another better if they acknowledged one another (we are so busy now, it is a wonder family members know each other by name).

At first it was awkward, not talking. When we all would walk to the dining hall separated from the retreat house by a long, narrow sidewalk through the trees, we were not sure how to do this: do we walk side by side? In a line? Stagger? How far apart? It seemed we collectively and silently decided to walk like ants, one after another. This way we didn't feel silly walking next to one another and not talking about the weather (which in itself seems silly).

Another thing about silence is you begin to hear differently. You notice how loud people are, especially on cell phones. And laughter is spontaneous. Since we are silent, we don't "choose" to laugh, but when you open your little morning cereal box like in kindergarten and it explodes three feet into the air, covering your head and entire table in Frosted Flakes like hoar frost, the laughter explodes from the deep recesses of your being and you feel exuberated and not a bit embarrassed.

Silence ultimately for a group of men who preach day in and day out, allows the mind to rest, the body to be at peace, and the capacity to identify the Lord in His Whisper.

Silence is a good thing. Indispensable for the body and soul. Words, like private property, are to be respected. And speaking of private property, what about the blanket? That will have to wait until the next article. In the meantime, let's keep silent and perhaps acknowledge it with only a nod.

It took about five days at the silent retreat before it happened: the desire to talk. The pattern of our day consisted of eating, praying, walking, praying, and eating. The only conversations between the priests were nods and grunts, except when a young priest spilled his glass of water at my table. He was so embarrassed and kept apologizing, then apologized for talking, then apologized again for the mishap.

Every diocesan priest is required by the Code of Canon Law to attend a weeklong retreat every year. I'll let you in on a little secret: most of us don't. Oh, we might take off a week for a retreat at the diocesan retreat center or somewhere else but Canon Law says a week, seven days. We arrive generally Monday night. Tuesday and Wednesday we try as best as we can to enter into the spirit of the retreat. Keep quiet. Pray. Walk and converse with the Lord.

On Thursday, about 1:00 in the afternoon, our thoughts drift back to the parish and when we will leave the retreat. Thursday afternoon, evening and Friday morning consists of making to do lists, mentally packing, and working on the homily for the upcoming Sunday. Prior to the morning Mass on Friday, the car is already packed, our sheets taken off the bed, and when Mass is over, we're gone!

In actuality our required week long retreat consists of two or three days.

On my recent eight day retreat, I wondered why I was receiving so many graces on this retreat and failed at others. As men, we generally like to be in charge, even if away. Being far away helps. As priests, we are concerned about our flock. Taking quality time away from the flock is an act of faith: faith in our people, our staff, and in God Himself.

Saint Augustine wrote in a time before e-mails, cars, or cell phones. As a priest and bishop he found it difficult to retreat but realized how important it was.

He wrote, "Let us leave a little room for reflection in our lives. Leave room for periods of silence and enter into ourselves; leave behind all noise and confusion...let us hear the Word of God in stillness and perhaps we may come to understand." (Sermon 52, 22) Even in the fourth century there was need for silence and reflection.

I love silence. People talk too much. When asked "How are you?" they really don't want to know, they are just nodding at you, acknowledging you, being polite. I find myself saying silly things to people because I often simply don't know what to say.

After five days of silence, I was ready to talk and had to wait three more days. What did I want to say? I wanted to share with someone how the Lord was speaking to me. What He was saying. What insights and consolations I was receiving. I wanted to share my experience with someone like a spouse would want to share his or her experiences while away from their loved one. When a priest returns from a good retreat, he feels the same way, and his spouse, the parish benefits!

So the next time your parish priest says he is going on retreat, thank him. Encourage him to take a full week. Tell him to take all the time God wants of him because in the end, everyone benefits.

Oh, I suppose you are wondering about the blanket I stole. The one I told you about last time? Remember this retreat consisted of: silence, eight days, and men. Well, the first night I got to the retreat house and bedded down for the night, I realized the heat was not on in the building. Old steam heat system.

It would be a long week, shivering in the cold without sleep. Penance is one thing, common sense is another. Asked to keep silence, I wasn't comfortable asking someone for a blanket. Plus it would make me look like a wimp. As a man who doesn't ask for directions or help, I quietly, stealthily snuck into the hall, slowing opening doors, knowing there had to be a linen closet somewhere.

After finding the broom closet, the stuffed storage room (if you build it, they will fill it!), I finally found the linen closet. One blanket. Very pink!

Settling into a warm bed finally, I drifted off to sleep with the glow of the hot pink blanket reflecting off the walls of the white washed room telling God: 'I think I should keep silent about this!'

I had a problem. I didn't know what to wear. An odd problem for a priest who wears black clerics every day symbolizing ashes. Other Catholics wear such symbolism once a year on Ash Wednesday signifying they are living for heaven, not earth.

For a series of eight mornings I did not don my usual garb of clerics, but dressed in "normal street" clothes, for an eight day silent retreat at Mundelein Seminary. Many of the priests wore their clerics or habits, others used the opportunity to dress in Dockers and sneakers, since we were cloistered with no one to ask if it's our day off (the usual question asked when people see me in street clothes coming from the gym or a walk in the woods).

This created a quandary. What to wear? Socks were easy being a black or white kind of guy (no pun intended). I went with black since men who wear white tube socks are unfashionable except at the gym, but I can't really keep up. In the past women wore socks that stopped at the ankle, now men are wearing them. "Anklets" they call them. Even the name sounds girlish. As for the shoes, I selected black sneakers. There seems to be a pattern forming.

Now more difficult choices. Beginning from feet up, I continued, pants: black, green (khaki I think they call it) or a tan white (I think they call that khaki too...confusing). I went for the green. Something different. Anytime you see a man with black shoes, black socks, black pants, and a dress shirt, you can be pretty certain he is a priest trying to not look like a priest even though everyone knows he is a priest. Among brother priests this is called "the priest on vacation look." It fools no one.

The green pants selected, what about a shirt? I choose a green shirt. Putting it on, I looked into the mirror. I looked like a 5'10" green zucchini. A nice looking zucchini, but none the less, a zucchini. Off went the green shirt.

Searching deeper into the closet, I choose a reddish shirt with bits of white wisps in it. I am not certain men should wear shirts with any sort of "wisps" in it, but decided to give it a go. Glancing at the mirror after brushing my teeth, I realized my entire outfit needed something brown, like a brown belt, to make me look like a hamburger between lettuce and tomato. Off went that shirt.

Digging now into the drawer I see a white and blue striped shirt. In the back of my mind I hear a voice, either my mother's or sister's (probably my sister) saying: "Never mix blue with something or you will look like a geek." (Yup, my sister's voice) But for the life of me, I can't remember what that "something" is not to mix with blue. (Or maybe it was brown? Where are Granimals when you need them?)

Looking further into my wardrobe, consisting of everything fitted in a carry-on bag, I realized I was running out of options, until I saw the deep recess of the closet.

"Perfect!" I thought. Grabbing the white and blue striped shirt I put it on, and over my ensemble I wrapped my black coat, hopefully covering any wardrobe malfunction, embarrassing my family and bishop. Suddenly the bells at the Church were ringing announcing the first conference had begun.

Thoughts immediately went to what I would wear the next day. This picking out clothes everyday surfaces many questions, such as: what is khaki? Who makes these rules? And most importantly: Should I wear the green pants two days in a row, or stagger them with the tan pants giving the impression I have a different outfit for each day.

This picking out clothes is a real monster! It's no wonder people are late for Mass. Next time I think I will wear my clerics, except that seems to make you a magnet for the TSA. Simply clothing yourself in Christ should be enough (Galatians 3:27). If we all would remember in heaven we are clothed by our good deeds (Ps. 132:9), we might not worry about what we wear on earth, and worry more about being naked in the afterlife.

Report from Retreat Number Four: Separated brethren in the same church

Eight days of a silent retreat? What did you do? A question asked often of priests who each year spend at least a week in retreat.

I was surprised how busy I was. After rising we prayed an hour. Ate breakfast in silence except for Frosted Flake's explosions (previous article reference); Spiritual direction, a time to talk with a more wise and experienced pray-er. A short walk followed by the celebration of Mass and lunch.

The afternoons consisted of an hour's walk around the lake watching the squirrels prepare for winter, then another hour's prayer in the seminary chapel filled with all the smells and creaks of an old 1920's church. Eucharistic Adoration followed by dinner then evening prayer, a conference about some spiritual matter such as thanksgiving; then a final hour of prayer and bed.

It was a time of separation from cell phones, internet, television, work and responsibilities. At the end we gathered and shared what happened. For some it was refreshing but for others it was difficult; constantly antsy, ready to do something. I experienced both.

The second day I went into the chapel and thought, "Good! I am alone here." Only five minutes passed when I heard the door open behind me. The wood floors creaked as a person genuflected and searched for a place to sit.

With only a few hundred places to choose from, with every groan of the floor, I wondered what was taking him so long to find a place. Slowly, with each step creaking on the wood floor, I soon realized out of a hundred choices to sit in this Cathedral sized chapel, the intruder (this was how I was feeling about him by this time) found his way near me.

'Surely not!' I thought. Surely so! Right behind me he knelt. 'Okay,' I was thinking, 'I can handle this. We are all part of the Body of Christ. He and I are children of the same God, brothers in the priesthood of Christ. If I cannot accept this person sitting near me to pray to the same Heavenly Father I am praying to, then there is something wrong with me!'

Soon I realized there was something wrong with me. After ten minutes of hearing the "child of God" behind me sneezing, sniffling, and snorting, I decided the "Body of Christ" would praise the Father better being separated from one another by some distance.

Tactfully getting up, I acted as if I was going to pray the Stations of the Cross and thought, 'Might as well pray them!' Afterwards I sat in different location, far from the child of God with a runny nose and no Kleenex. Separated brethren we were, but at least in the same church!

I felt anxious. Past memories, future events, present worries flooded my mind making it difficult to pray. The silence and solitude of a retreat can surface many feelings. A spiritual director or guide is necessary for the journey. In an introductory meeting my spiritual director suggested I clear my mind of unnecessary distraction. God had plans to fill me with His Grace. All that was necessary was to be open. As with all good advice, I knew he was right. But "how" was the question.

The weather finally changed and was becoming warm and as I sat there, with the snorting child of God across the church, I began to get hot. Looking to my side, I noticed the window was open. 'Strange,' I thought, 'with the window open, why am I so hot?'

Looking closer at the window, I realized it was in fact open, but the outside storm window was tightly shut. The floor beneath my feet popped and creaked as I walked to the window and opened the storm window. Fresh air flooded in.

Going back to my seat amidst the fresh flowing air, I settled into the pew and reflected on what happened. I intended to be open to God's grace during this retreat. Perhaps there is a storm window still closed in my soul not allowing God to flow.

A good snort across the church took my thoughts to other "children of God" whom I had separated myself from, although in the same church. The grace of the retreat then began for me. The longer I remained focused on my response to God's acceptance of me, the more I was able to accept others in my life. As I did so, the snorting seemed to quiet and I rested in God's spirit.

Getting up, I thanked God for the hour's prayer experience in that Cathedral like chapel, and leaving the church nodded to my brother priest in obvious distress with a head cold. The storm window of my soul was opened.

118

The death of a priest (Part One)

It was one of those phone calls you dread. When the conversation begins, "I am really sorry to have to tell you this over the phone," you know it's not good news. A few weeks ago, I received such a call. The caller was informing me of the death of a close priest friend of mine in Pennsylvania. A priest for over 35 years, my friend was only 61 years old. Entirely too young and totally unexpected.

He contracted the flu. Unable to shake it, he died. I had the notion only elderly die of the flu. Not too many years ago, 61 might have been considered elderly; not today. But death doesn't discriminate between old and young, rich or poor, priest or laity. It is our remedy to see God face to face.

"You are not here to be remembered." An older priest surprised me once by saying after a priest friend of his died, when I commented about the lack of people at the funeral. I thought he was being rather calloused. After moving from assignment to assignment, I understand. A former pastor becomes *"Father What's His Name,"* in about two years. It's natural.

When a priest dies, he leaves no children, no spouse, and no dependents. If he has been retired for a time, his funeral mourners consist of brother priests and a few laity. Often heard among people reading a priest's obituary is, "Where was he at? Oh, I never heard of him."

As priests, we are popes of our county or sometimes block, known only to the people we serve, and not always by them. Recently I experienced this when I ventured to speak at a meeting outside of any parish boundaries I served. Having been ordained over twenty years, I was surprised to be asked an innocent question inquiring whether I had ever served in a parish. (The best part was when they asked me how much younger I was than their pastor... I'm a good 10 years older!)

All priests want to be active to the very end. This is how my friend died. He was very active. Went to World Youth Day's all over the world and recently began a ministry in Haiti, providing spiritual and medical assistance to a sister parish.

Being still in active ministry, his funeral was packed to overflowing. The suddenness and shock gathered his entire flock to attend his funeral Mass. Too bad we can't do the same for our retired priests and religious. Understandable, but too bad.

I remember another older priest, surprised me by commenting about the death of a priest friend of his. "That's the way to go!" he said, "What way" I naively asked. "On a Sunday morning!" He replied with a glint in his eye.

I pushed him to clarify, and he explained: 'When a priest is called by the Lord to go home on a Saturday night or Sunday morning before Sunday Masses, the parish is gathered for Sunday Mass, and no Father. They go look for him and then come running to the church exclaiming that Father has died. The entire congregation falls to their knees and offers up a rosary for his soul, right then and there. Beautiful!'

How do priests deal with the death of another priest? I've lost friends, a parent, family, but the sorrow felt at the death of a brother priest is unlike others. A priest to another priest is a brother, a father, a mentor, a friend, a confidant. The closest comparison might be of a spouse. We priests share a bond with one another that we don't share with anyone else.

This bond is forged by the unique role we play of bringing Christ into the world, by forgiving other's their sins, by offering eternal life through the waters of baptism. It is forged by the distinctive attacks of Satan upon us, similar to the temptations Jesus experienced after being called by the Father, my Beloved. The fraternity, community, and relationships among priests are unique; therefore the sorrow at the loss of such a relationship is distinctive.

"You are not here to be remembered." While on the face of it harsh words, we priests wouldn't want it any other way. At our ordination we died to Christ, so that Christ might live in us. If mourners came to our funeral because of us, we were ineffective in our ministry to the Lord. But if they came to give God thanks and praise for the ministry of a priest who brought them to an intimate and lasting relationship with the Lord, then we can truly be laid in peace, where God's knowledge is all in all.

For all the priests of our diocese and in our lives who have gone before us, marked with the sign of our Faith, may their good deeds go before them, and may they continue to intercede for us as they did on earth. May they also rest in His peace.

The death of a priest (Part Two)

In the seminary was a phrase among seminarians that was both joke and reality. It was "The ribbon check." Seminarians are taught to pray the Liturgy of the Hours. When ordained a deacon, prior to priesthood, he accepts the obligation of praying the Liturgy of the Hours daily for the rest of his life.

The Liturgy of the Hours consists of five different "offices" or "hours." They are: Office of Readings, Morning Prayer, Mid-Day Prayer, Evening Prayer, and Night Prayer. As the day progresses the ribbon marking the different "offices" or prayers advance. As the days turn into weeks, the ribbon should march forward...forward, that is, if the owner of the book is praying!

A seminarian might find himself before his spiritual director saying, "I don't think God wants me to be a priest." A wise spiritual director will then ask to see the young man's breviary (prayer book) for a "ribbon check." Often vocational crisis coincide with stationary ribbons.

Or a brother seminarian will come into your room, see your breviary sitting on your bed or desk, and to possibly embarrass you, will call out: "Ribbon check!" Grabbing your breviary, he will check and see if your ribbons are set to the right day and correct hour. If they are not, good natural ribbing ensues, not to mention some fraternal correction and embarrassment.

In the seminary we would kid one another wondering what would happen if we died and coming to our bedroom, would they find our ribbons up to date, or find them woefully behind? At the time, being young and ingenious, we thought we could start a service to cover any embarrassment in case you were prone to not keep up with your prayers.

The service would consist of this: when you die, someone would get to your room first, set the ribbons on the correct day and correct hour. This way when you were found, all would be in order! Perfect! (Of course we were not thinking about what the Good Lord might think about all of this)

Recently a good priest friend of mine passed away suddenly at the young age of 61. He died in his parish rectory from complications of the flu. After working through the shock of his death, I began to think of what he left behind. I wondered who would take care of his dog, Noah. (Priests always seem to name their pets after Biblical characters. Mine is a combination of the Bible and a John Wayne movie. Says a bit about me huh?)

I also wondered what my friend's parishioners found left behind in his office, home, etc. What was he working on before he died. His life being interrupted, I speculated what remnants remained would enlighten others what was essential to him. I also wondered about his ribbons!

Having had the privilege of serving as the Vicar of Clergy for the Diocese, I've entered priest's home after death. What we leave out, leave mid completed, and leave behind says much about what was important to us in this life.

One such priest's apartment was sparse. Having been moved to the nursing home, he took only what was important. When I entered, I saw a huge television with a statue of Our Lady on top of it. 'Obviously television was important to him; living here, it must have given him some much needed entertainment', I thought to myself until I saw the large television was unplugged, and the unused remote in a drawer. No doubt the television was a gift from a well-meaning family member or former parishioner, but for the priest, it served only as an altar for the statue of Our Lady overlooking his bed and room.

The most memorable "leavings behind" was of one of our priest who was active to the end. As his items were gathered for his funeral, all of which were neatly laid out by the deceased priest, a piece of paper was noticed in his manual typewriter. Contained on the paper were daily entries of comments and reflections on the Gospel of the day.

Even though he no longer served a parish or gave a daily homily, here in his last years, he continued to meditate, reflect, and write homilies on the daily Mass readings. Looking at the last entry, you can guess what was found: it was dated the day before his death. To the end, he faithfully proclaimed the Gospel.

I don't know what they found at my friends home. For me, I re-read some of his recent e-mails to me. One, dated six days before his death was reflecting on a movie about St. Teresa of Avila. Finding much to think about from the movie, he wrote: "So much to learn. So little time." I am certain his ribbons were correctly positioned.

God allows us the time we need to keep our ribbons in order. Look around you. If the Lord called you home at this moment, what would you leave behind? If we live each moment as if it's our first moment in eternity with God, then what we leave behind will show it.

The Solace of a Cemetery

Since beginning these articles titled, "The View from the Rectory Window," I've noticed fewer and fewer people driving by my rectory window. Probably because they don't want to end up in one of my articles! Even some of my priest friends have threatened me if I include them in an article. I live on the edge! But the view I have from the rectory window is different now.

Being the director for the Diocesan retreat house my view from my rectory window is of my future. From my window facing north, I look to the west and see my immediate future: the priest retirement apartments. To the east, I see my eventual future, Ascension Cemetery. Not everyone has a glimpse of their future out the window. I live between my two futures.

These two views have afforded me to see a number of happenings. To the east, Ascension Cemetery, I've been intrigued by the different scenes of the seemingly same drama, grief. In the privacy of a cemetery, one finds both peace and anger, solace and exasperation, but most of all, questions whose intellectual answers must be felt, in order to be realized.

On my walk through the cemetery in the evening, I noticed a woman about my age. She nods as she drives by, and I with rosary in hand, lift a hand in greeting. I don't know if she realizes I am a priest. I am not really certain she even really sees me. Rarely does a day go by when I either see her on my walk or out my window.

Parking her car, she briskly walks to a grave midway up the slight sloping hill. Standing as a sentinel, silhouetting against the early evening sky, she stops at a grave for only a moment or two. Adjusting the flowers or picking a bit of grass around the headstone, she turns and heads for her car and exits the cemetery.

As I continue my rosary exercise walk, trying to merge raising my heart rate for bodily benefit, and raising my heart to the Lord for spiritual benefit, I become curious and cannot shake wondering whose grave the woman is visiting. Is it her mother, a child, or spouse? Perhaps a grandparent. No, a daily trip, it must be someone very close to her.

It's really none of my business.   A cemetery is a private place, where one can grieve alone in its stillness. Being with one through the process of death, then participating in the rosary vigil, the funeral, the internment, the funeral dinner, all of these are filled with people and voices. It is a blur, creating a surreal experience, leaving us afterwards wondering who was there and what was said.

It is only after we have placed our loved one in their resting place to wait for the Lord to raise them from the dead and we begin healing; it is in these holy places the human voices cease and the voice of God can finally be heard.

After the woman leaves, curiosity gets the best of me, and I walk to the grave she visits. It is that of a younger man who passed away three years ago. He was in his early 50's. My mind wraps around this information and my imagination is liberated in wonder. He must be her husband. I wonder if they have children. I wonder how he was taken so young. I wonder how his family is doing. I wonder...

Walking again, now with a new purpose of reciting the rosary, I begin to pray for the woman, the man, and any family. Feeling at first guilty for having allowed my curiosity to lead me to the grave and intrude on the woman's grief, I now feel reassured having an understanding and new purpose of my prayer walks through the cemetery. Now as I look at other grave markers, allowing the Holy Spirit to guide me, I pray for these different peoples, families, and situations.

This is what being a priest is about. Observing, being present, participating, even at a distance, and praying. The woman is obviously grieving the absence of her husband. She also is a woman of faith to keep returning to tend a grave with such love and affection. I would imagine her faith is being tested by her grief, but it is in grief we are found by God. It is in grief we seek out places, such as cemeteries, to find His quiet, and to experience what we know to be true, but to be able to ask anyway.

"Woman, why are you weeping? Who are you looking for?"

Then Jesus said to her, "Mary!"

From the Cross to the Easter Bunny

It was a simple question really, but the question contained more layers than realized by the person seeking an answer. Such is the life of a parish priest, or a parent for that matter.

"Can we have an Easter egg hunt after Mass?" Simple. Straightforward. Well meaning. The Knights of Columbus were the one's requesting. The purpose of such a hunt was to allow families to come together and celebrate Easter. Thankfully, and rather oddly, they requested to have the hunt on Passion/Palm Sunday.

"No," I said, "Palm Sunday is not the appropriate time for such an event." Since they were unable to coordinate a rabbit egg hunt on Easter Sunday, I breathed a sigh of relief. I was off the hook. This time.

As a priest I live in a different world. I realize this. The world I live in is the world of the Church with Her calendar and understanding of the world. The Knights and other parishioners have the more complicated job of living in the secular world, where the secular and the sacred are mixed, and original meanings are forgotten.

A well-meaning event sponsored by a tremendously supportive group of the parish is difficult to turn down. Had timing not been the issue, I would have been left in a difficult position for my homily was already prepared for Easter Sunday.

My homily read as follows:

"He stood on bare ground, completely naked, bloody, and resolute. They offer wine mixed with gall. Gall, a poisonous bile from the liver which deadens pain. It is a narcotic. Refusing the concoction, His bloody body is stretched onto wood, hammering nails through His flesh fastening His body onto the wood until they would later remove the lifeless body from the nails.

After three excruciating hours He gasped and died. Onlookers after humiliating Him, yelling at Him, and sarcastically ridiculing Him, went home to another ordinary Friday evening in which for two thousand years is seen as the most extraordinary Friday in the history of the world.

Three days later, really 39 hours later, women came to the burial place to finish the burial rite and they found it empty. Incredible events are then recorded: He appears talking, eating, and alive. Unbelievable for some, a matter of faith for others, and a time of decision for even others.

So what happened? How did we get from a bloody, naked, brutal execution and the joy of the resurrection to cute little bunny laying chicken eggs? How did we get from the most important three days of the universe to an Anglo-Saxon earthly fertility symbol? What happened?

What happened? We let it happen. We <u>are</u> letting it happen! We are no different than Peter denying Jesus when we deny we are Christians at work, at school, in our nation's politics.

We are no different than the apostles watching at a safe distance as Jesus was mocked on the cross when we fail to receive the Lord in the Eucharist, forgiveness in Confession or marriage in a sacrament.

We are no different than Thomas who says, "Show me!" when we attempt to create heaven on earth rather than seeing our earthly lives as a way of achieving heaven.

But today we can make a difference! We can make a new choice. A new beginning. A resurrection.

Easter is not about fertility rites. Easter is not about egg hunts. Easter is about our Catholic faith. Our belief that there is something beyond this earthly life. Easter is about the triumph over suffering and death.

On Ash Wednesday we were marked with ashes. A remembrance that "Death is assured, and life on earth is short," but life after this vale of tears is eternal and assured for those who have faith in the cross and resurrection of Jesus Christ.

Unbelievable for some. A matter of faith for others. And perhaps a time of decision for even others today.

Which are we going to follow: The Cross here on earth to a resurrection in the kingdom of God, or an elusive mythical hare? The choice is ours."

It is difficult living in the secular world while trying to remain sacred. Thankfully the Knights were unable to pull off an Easter egg hunt this year. Now all I have to do is figure how to convince them not to have their golf tournament on the Lord's Day of Sunday. Ahh, the life of a pastor!

Serving Christ in ordinary ways

Generally when I arrive, I rearrange the chairs so a person seated behind me can speak into my ear unseen. Or a person can sit in front of me and face to face experiencing the forgiveness the Lord wishes offers in the Sacrament of Confession at a parish penance service.

The chair behind me, I prefer to set in a manner I can best hear the penitent. If they choose to be anonymous, often they will whisper in an inaudible whisper, requiring me to lean back farther in my chair to understand them.

The chair in front, I place two leg's length before me at a comfortable distance. Inevitably the chair seems to germinate more than its' four legs, and slowly creeps closer to me, only to have me push it back to its proper place when a penitent leaves. I like some distance between us. That whole personal space thing.

Recently I was driving to a parish penance service. Skipping the dinner beforehand knowing from experience there is nothing worse than eating a famously hefty meal, then sitting in a confessional for two hours.

As I was driving, listening to the Bible, a great way to meditate while driving, I was listening about the separation of the sheep from the goats at the last judgment (Matthew 25:31-46). A passage which describes the spiritual and corporeal works of mercy: "For I was hungry and you gave me food..." A passage I often use to explain that stewardship is the sharing of our gifts and being of Christ to one another. A passage which I often am uncomfortable hearing.

It might seem odd to you I find this passage so difficult to hear, but as I hear the words I am reminded and challenged. Wondering what group I belong.

I consider the manager of a local food diner for those in need, and how I am often asked, "Hey Father, we would love to see you helping us?" Or I remember the years I assisted in completing paperwork for an organization helping people stay in their homes and out of homeless shelters. As much as I would like, I cannot any longer give much time for such a worthy cause.

But I am a priest, not ordained to serve a computer screen! How can I <u>not</u> assist the poor, the hungry, the homeless? What kind of preacher am I who cannot even take an afternoon out of a week and serve the poor? All my needs are taken care of by the Church. How can I be so selfish?

The more I considered the passage the more uncomfortable I became, thinking about priests who go to Haiti or Mexico to build houses or distribute medicine, I thought maybe I could do something like that. No, I can't hammer nails straight, and I only speak English. Why couldn't I be a better priest?

With all of these thoughts ruminating within me, I sulked through the Penance Service, not wanting to fully participate. Not feeling worthy.

Going to my assigned place, I rearranged the chairs in my usual way. As I put my weight down into the chair, a cushy chair provided, for we wouldn't want Father not be comfortable, my first penitent arrived.

As expected upon arrival, up comes the chair so close to me they could hold my hands. I recoiled into my cushy chair trying to establish some personal space. Leaning forward towards me, negating any personal space I established, they said: "Father, I like to go to confession face to face if that's alright. I love coming to confession face to face, because then I can see the face of Christ who forgives my sins."

Like lightning out of a blue sky, God shook me. This is how I am to be Christ. Feeding the hungry, sheltering the homeless, and the other works of mercy are important, but I have been called to be in the person of Christ through the gifts of the priesthood: forgiving sins, consecrating the bread and wine into the Body and Blood of Christ, proclaiming the Good News of the Gospel. This penitent is the Christ I am to serve.

The mere fact I was driving to another town to hear confessions is missionary work, albeit not Haiti or Mexico, but just as vital. Just being who I am and doing what I do is enough, if I do it as Christ would.

I suspect many a parent, grandparent, teacher, police officer, or anyone who serves others understood this long ago. Feeding the hungry and sheltering the homeless is serving the person in need right in front of you with the gifts given. And that person might even be your son or daughter, or parishioner. We don't have to travel across the world to serve Christ. We can serve Christ in our ordinary lives in seemingly ordinary ways.

The Personal File

At every parish I begin a file. This file is not for budgets or building projects nor homilies. This file is what I mark the "personal file."

The file looks ordinary. A manila folder with a tab labeled "Personal." Contained inside are letters and notes from parishioners who took the time to write a card or letter explaining how God worked through the priesthood I've been given. This file looks ordinary, but it can be a lifeline.

I began this file as a newly ordained priest and it has served me well. Like everyone, I can receive comments, but for every ten comments or letters received, there will be one not so complimentary, or even nasty. Being a person who desires to be accepted, I forget the other nine flattering letters or comments and focus on the critical one.

Critical letters often center upon sports, uniform policy, or discipline of children in PSR or school. Sometimes, but rarely, they center upon a homily or theological point. Often though they are in response to some instance where I placed my foot into my mouth.

Critical letters can be divided into three categories: Stealth bombers, PBM's, and Trojan Horses.

Some critical letters arrive anonymous. These are what I call the Stealth Bombers. I've learned not to read or even open them. It is frustrating and often useless in not being able to respond to their concern. When e-mail first became standard but still new, I would receive a few stealth or "anonymous e-mails" from folks who didn't realize their e-mail address of metildasmith@yahooo.com pulled back the curtain of anonymity.

Some comments have arrived by registered mail. Now there is tenacity! These I call PBM's, precision guided munitions. To send a letter by registered mail, the person wanted to make certain it fell into the right hands. These are rare, but still part of the arsenal.

Finally there is the Trojan Horse letter. The beginnings are civil and even flattering, and then Wham! Just when you think all is well, there is a "but Father…" Frequently these letters are written by well-meaning parishioners who desire to be respectful but have a complaint or suggestion.

It is important for parishioners to voice their thoughts and complaints. I've learned a great deal from critical letters about how I can appear un-Christ like. Saint Paul cautioned the younger priest Timothy, "Take great care about what you do and what you teach; always do this, and in this way you will save both yourself and those who listen to you." (1 Timothy 4:16) Being a priest comes with many hazards, such as taking oneself too seriously or misusing one's authority.

Soon after ordination, after the honeymoon was over, and the pink glasses were misplaced, I realized the need to begin a "personal" folder. In this folder are some wonderful letters, cards, and notes of how God worked through me in spite of, or because of my weaknesses.

One of the first letters I received was from a young man in high school. Hospitalized for several months with painful intestinal spasms. I did nothing really. Sat with him in his hospital room and listened to music with him. Talked and prayed with him. But after he recovered he sent me a gracious note thanking me for being there for him. It went into the personal file.

Then there the woman who called me one evening to the nursing home for her mother. Dutifully I went, but grumbling. It wasn't my parishioner. Complaining to myself that I must be the only priest who doesn't have voice mail and answers the phone (poor me!), I entered the room.

The family was gathered. It would prove to be the last hours of the woman's life. Thinking she was comatose, I was surprised when she began to pray the Our Father with us while anointing her. Ashamed for the way I felt on my drive to the home, I left with a renewed understanding of why I am a priest, and very thankful I was available to come. There is nothing worse than to be taught to always call a priest when a loved one is dying and not to be able to get a hold of one. I was humbled.

But more humbled a month or so later when a note arrived which said, "As our family stood with you, we afterwards realized we were experiencing one of the most spiritually moving events of our lives."

What a great privilege it is to be a priest, even when I don't always realize it!

Yes, it's important to learn from one's mistakes, but it's also important to remember and repeat one's successes. As Saint Paul wrote, "Rejoice always, pray continually, and give thanks in all circumstances; for this is God's will for you in Christ Jesus." (1 Co. 5: 17-18)

I think everyone should have a personal file.

"If there is no resurrection of the dead, then not even Christ has been raised. 14 And if Christ has not been raised, our preaching is useless and so is your faith."

-Saint Paul's first letter to the Corinthians, Chapter 15: 13-14

Of maintenance men and priests and "the look"

It was a familiar look. One of those patronizing looks.
Perhaps it's not virtuous to say but, I'm not stupid... I don't
think so anyway. The virtue of humility would dictate I
respond to "the look" with appreciation and meekness. I
don't do very well with that.

What predicated "the look" and the accompanying
question was an innocent inquiry on my part.

Entering the daily Mass chapel on a warm day in July, I
immediately knew something was wrong. It was hot. Really
hot. Going over to the thermostat, I saw it read over 80
degrees. After making certain the air conditioner was on, set
at the proper setting and temperature, I went to find our
maintenance man knowing the evening Mass goers would
appreciate some air conditioning.

"Ray?" I said after seeing him in the main church, "Hey the
small chapel is hot...really hot. Anything you can do about it?"

Then the question that precedes "the look, "Weelll,
Father. (They drag out the well) Did you check the
thermostat?" Now "the look!"

"The look" is a patronizing, "Gee are you really that dumb"
look. It says, "Okay college boy, do I have to do everything for
you?" Holding back my egotism, I replied in my most
pleasant voice, "Yes Ray. It's set on 'ac.'

"Did you check the temperature?" He followed up. Gulping I replied, "Yes, it's set on 70. But still nothing." With a profound breath, Ray moved slowly towards the daily Mass chapel, and after checking the thermostat, Ray explained what could be the problem.

"It could be a loss of pressure in the evaporator coil that means the refrigerant is colder than the temperature of the dew point. When the air conditioner or heat evaporator is below the dew point, the humidity will freeze the coil. Frost forms and then glazes over the air conditioner evaporator coil.

Or it could be if the AC evaporator coil pan, drain line, or drain pan is clogged. If so there are a couple of ways I could use to free up the line. Use a CO_2 gun to blow the line using cartridges, which provides high pressure blowing out the line of algae or whatever else, is clogging the line. This lets the moisture to drain. But sometimes the drain has to be cut and replaced after being blown, so only certified professionals can do this, so we would have to call someone. Or I could use a high pressure nitrogen, a water pipe or a shop vacuum to do this."

I felt like I was being schooled by *Tool Time Tim* of *Home Improvements*. I hate it when they do this! "Ray," I interrupted, "look into it and let me know. Thanks."

This is so typical of the maintenance men I work with in a parish. It drives me nuts. They think I'm an idiot when it comes to maintenance things.

So when I arrived at a new parish and the former pastor explained there was a television antenna on the roof, and all I needed to do was to move the antenna line from his old bedroom to my new bedroom, for about ten seconds I thought of asking the maintenance man to do this. I knew he could do it in a flash, but overcome with overconfidence I thought, "No, this is something anyone, including me, can do. I'm not an idiot!"

First I had to find the crawlspace entrance in the ceiling. After finding the entrance an hour later, I had to find a ladder. Another hour later I was set. Carefully I climbed the ladder reflecting how numerous and difficult it was to fill out the insurance forms for accidents on the parish property.

With insurance paperwork on my mind, I cautiously placed one foot over another onto the studs vigilant not to step through the ceiling. Climbing through the jumble of rafters, air conditioner duct work, and insulation I found myself lost in the maze, not certain what room I was standing over and regretting I did not change out of my black clerics now covered with pink insulation. (Just picture the pink panther with a clerical collar)

Finally success! I found the antenna on the roof and followed the cord carefully to the hole in the ceiling. With care I began to haul the cord to pull it up from the room into the attic so I could transfer it over to my new bedroom.

All went well until I felt a weight at the end of the antenna cord. I must be caught on something, I thought, so I tugged harder. Wham! I heard, while all the cord I previously pulled through the ceiling hole recoiled downward.

What could that possibly be? I thought as I retracted my steps through the maze of insulation, ductwork and rafters. Walking into the room, I realized my error.

There in the center of the room hung a flat screen television, dangling mid-air on the end of the antenna cord I was attempting to pull through the ceiling! I forgot to unfasten the TV!

Sheepishly looking around and thankful I live only with an old dog who keeps my secrets, I could see the ghostly image of my former maintenance man Ray, shaking his head, giving me "the look" and saying, "Weelll... Father..."

I really hate that look.

"Pray, Hope, and Don't Worry"
-St. Pio of Pietrelcino

The unique fatherhood of a priest

Turning, seeing black pants and knees at eye level, the little boy instinctually raised his hands and whimpered, "Daddy!" Looking about, I saw large groups of families in the church's gathering space, but no Daddy... except me. Knowing a response was expected from the teary eyed child, I reached down and picked up the toddler and brought him up to my shoulder.

Looking surprised that the face next to his was not "his" Daddy, he didn't seem to mind, and buried his wet face into my shoulder. With my hand on the back of his head, I swayed slightly and spoke softly into his ear. He quieted down.

After a moment, a voice next to me said, "He seems to like you!"

The boy's head jerked towards the voice. With arms outstretched the boy cried "Daddy!" and an exchange was made from one father to another.

I can't say this happens all the time, but often enough to know what it feels like to comfort a child who mistakes me for his father. And in fact the child is really not mistaken. "From the lips of children and infants you have brought forth praise (Mt. 21:16)." It is from children that profound theological insights are made and weighty questions are asked.

Catholics realize a priest is called "Father" because we have been committed to the priest's spiritual care. Just as a father cares, nurtures, and protects his family, so a priest, especially a pastor, cares, nurtures, and protects his flock. This filial affection and respect is vocalized in the salutation "Father." It is an informal salutation rather than a title. The title for a priest is actually "Reverend" or "Reverend Father." But where did this salutation begin? A question children often ask.

Since the beginning, the Church used the title "Father" for religious leaders. First Bishops, the shepherds of the local church, were given the title "papa" until around the year 400. Papa of course means father. In English papa is rendered "pope."

Saint Benedict in the 6th century called spiritual confessors "Fathers" because they were the guardians of souls. The word "abbot," the leader of the monastery, is from the word "Abba," the Aramaic Hebrew word for father, but in a very familiar sense of "daddy."

By the Middle Ages the term "father" was used to address friars such as the Franciscans and Dominicans. The people saw by their teaching, preaching, and charitable works they were caring for the physical and spiritual needs of the people, just like a father with his children. Today in English speaking countries it is customary to call a priest "Father."

While the salutation or title comes with ordination, a priest grows into the role of a "father." I remember clearly my first couple of years after ordination, waking up on a Monday morning and thinking: 'Now I can be just me!'

It was my "day off," the proverbial sacred cow of a priest's week. I could put on my blue jeans and t-shirt and just "be me!" Little did I understand that "me" was now a father!

This is a natural progression of maturity. Young husbands and fathers experience this. "Now that I am away from the house, I can just be me!" or "Now that I am with the guys, I can be myself."

It is interesting to watch a young father or a young priest develop into the role of a father. God seems to have a sense of humor and stacks of patience! It normally doesn't take too long for the young man, priest or husband, to understand who he was, is no more. God has a new identity for him!

Do I miss comforting a child? Do I sometimes yearn for the intimacy of looking at a child, knowing I was co-responsible of bringing that soul into the world? Of course. I wouldn't be a good priest if I did not have these yearnings.

That being said, there is nothing compared to bringing a child into the world of grace as a child of God in the sacrament of baptism, or consecrating bread and wine to feed a child uniting them for the first time, body and soul with our Lord.

But the most important moment as a spiritual father is in the confessional, welcoming a child back into the grace of the Heavenly Father, whether that child is 10 or 90, it is both incredible and humbling. Like bringing a soul into God's world and His Kingdom, for "no greater joy can I have than this, to hear that my children follow the truth." (3 John 4)

Out of the mouths of children. Abba, Father!

148

Do not call anyone your father!

"From the lips of children and infants you have brought forth praise (Mt. 21:16)." It is from children profound theological insights are made and weighty questions others want to ask are asked.

Nate had a gleam in his eye. Such a gleam in an eighth grade boy is a sign of either having done something wrong or about to do something wrong. He raised his hand and said bluntly, "Do not call anyone on earth your father. Only one is your father, the One in heaven. Matthew 23:9.... So *Father* (exaggerated), why should I call you *father*?"

He thought he had me. I was playing a dangerous game with the eighth grade class I call "Stump Father!" based on the infamous radio show *Click and Clack Car* Talk show. In the show, they have a portion called *"Stump the Chump!"* where people try to stump them!

His question was a good one even if he was asking it for the wrong reasons. Feeling more and more like a father whose child has just asked where babies come; I draw a deep breath and answer, "Because that is who I am! Let me explain..."

The crux of understanding a priest as a father is that it is "who" I am, not "what" I am.

If we take the words of Jesus in Matthew 23:9 literally, we should not call anyone on earth our father, including our own dad. Jesus went onto so say not to anyone on earth Rabbi or

Teacher. Both of which Jesus was called, e.g., Mark 9:5, 10:51, John 1:38, etc.

When reading the Sacred Scriptures we must first remember the context of the passage. Taking a sound bite from a person and applying it can be deceiving of what the message really was.

Such "cherry picking" of verses can lead one into trouble. Take for instance the following New Testament quotes: "You blind guides! You strain out a gnat but swallow a camel." (Matthew 23:24) We know the Pharisees did not swallow a camel whole, but the point was they were more concerned about the little things than the bigger picture.

"Everything is possible to one who has faith." (Mark 9:23b) Yes, but what happens when one prays with genuine faith the bank you intend to rob has lots of money in it? Common sense tells us this is not what Jesus is talking about.

"If your right eye causes you to sin, tear it out and throw it away." (Matthew 5:29) Really? And finally, "If anyone comes to me without hating his father and mother, wife and children, brothers and sisters, and even his own life, he cannot be my disciple." (Luke 14:26) Yes, hate! Well, perhaps Luke got it wrong? No, Jesus was trying to make a point. You must love God before all other things!

These are called hyperboles. We use them all the time to make a point. "These books weigh a ton!" Meaning they are really heavy! "I could sleep for a year." Meaning I'm really tired! "I'm so hungry, I could eat a horse." Well, only in central Asia according to Wikipedia!

Jesus' use of such emphasis in not calling anyone on earth a rabbi, father, or teacher was to remind and even shock us into recognizing only God is our Father, rabbi, or teacher. We receive all our authority and who we are, only from God.

I often wonder what happened to Nate (not his real name). He had many, many questions and sometimes would frustrate me because I might know the answer, but be unable to articulate it. This is often the frustration a parent has with their children.

As a spiritual father I've learned I do not have all the answers. I am limited as a father. Only *Our Father* can fully have all the answers. It humbling not to be always right or have the right answer. This is what I think Jesus was saying when he said don't call anyone on earth your father, rabbi, or teacher.

So if you are a "Nate" out there, don't quit asking questions. It is in the seeking that you will find, and often the person you ask will learn too...even Father!

Ministering in the final hour

The gathering of people spilled out into the hallway. Sadness and concern etched on their faces, but also a sense of gratitude. Gratitude the pain would soon be over. Gratitude of a life given. Gratitude of our Catholic faith.

The small sea of family, friends, and parishioners parted as I walked into the small room. Although many did not know me, did not recognize my name, or have any connection to me, they parted giving me room to kneel down in prayer. They recognized I was a brother to the one I sought, and therefore a relative to them.

The one I sought and knelt before was lying on a bed. A bed not of his own until two months ago. A bed in which a month ago he sat and spoke with me with enthusiasm about a sporting game on the television and the approaching of his final hour. A bed in which he asked for my blessing, and I his. A bed upon which he would soon no longer need for he was making a transition from this life to another.

He that lay upon the bed was my brother. Although thirty-seven years my senior, nearly the age of what my father would have been, he and I still were brothers. We are both priests.

Walking into the room, filled with so many people, so many emotions, so many ages, my thoughts were scattered, vacillating between concern for the people and concern for the brother priest; between the wonderment of so many people whom he touched in his life gathered around him and wondering who would be gathered around me at my hour; vacillating between sorrow and joy.

Not remaining in such vacillation, I knelt before his willowy body and pressing my hand into his. Carefully placing the relic and cross of Saint Peregrine, the Cancer Saint, I reminded him and those present who Peregrine was and how his intercession along with the Blessed Virgin Mother's would pierce the heavenly clouds.

Unable to speak, my brother's voice from the past was resonated within my mind: "Hello Father!" "You're doing a great job, Father!" "Love those articles Father!"

Always he called me "Father." Even 37 years my senior and unnecessary among priests to be so formal, so official, and so proper. But his salutation was not of formality or etiquette, it was of respect. He was reminding me of my identity, and constantly encouraging my mission of proclaiming the Gospel, which came forth only because of my identity of being a "Father," a priest.

Praying from my heart, I spoke of how my brother priest lived his entire life to reach this moment, this hour. So many Hail Mary's he prayed which he petitioned Mary to pray for us, "now and at the hour of our death." It's interesting how many of us forget the purpose of our lives here on earth is to reach our hour, the hour of our death. We live as if we don't want to reach this hour, or won't.

I also thanked God for my brother's priesthood, and how his example of persona Christi modeled the priesthood for many of us. His attentiveness to the people, his unwavering voice proclaiming Gospel values and morals in a constantly changing culture, and his availability to hear confessions, especially of brother priests were all a pattern for us to live our priesthood.

Finishing praying, I heard a faint, but still resilient whisper, "Amen." He had heard me of which I was thankful. Slowly getting up, knowing I would not see him, with God's help, until the light of a new day in eternity, the family and friends parted once more.

Allowing me room to leave, and allowing them the space to both grieve and give thanks.

The priesthood. What a wonderful gift. A gift a man receives, and continues to give whether in the pulpit, altar, or deathbed. What a gift ministering to a brother priest in his final hour, and to be ministered to, in his final hour.

"All the darkness in the world cannot extinguish the light of a single candle."
-St. Francis

Those first steps

There she stood. Unwilling to move or budge. Nothing would move her. Not the crowd politely pushing her from behind. Nor the voice beckoning before her.

She was on the precipice of a new experience. Hanging on the edge of a cliff, wanting, but not fully willing to take the first step. She was afraid.

I was returning from a trip traveling by plane. At one leg of the journey was a short layover at the Denver airport. The 'glow worm' terminal, as it is fondly called, because the airport terminal from a distance looks like the child's toy "glow worm." A cute, cuddly stuffed worm when squeezed looks like a worm glowing. (Causing one to ponder the absurdity of children's toys which forever will cause a child to think worms glow and purple dinosaurs can dance.)

Walking through the airport I heard the odd combination of a frantic but amused cry of a mother, "Step! Take a step! It will be okay! Take a step!"

The child, a little girl probably 5 years old, was perched on the edge of the moving walkway. Obviously the little girl had never encountered a moving sidewalk, nor was she inclined to do so now. Even with the flow of people behind her trying to thrust her forward and the encouraging voice of her mother, she would not nudge.

Slowing down to watch the drama unfold, I was curious to see what would happen. Would the girl take the first forbidding step? Would the mother return to her daughter, walking against the current of people and the moving walkway? Would the encouragement of the older man on the adjacent walkway give her the bravery to take that first step?

It was evident the mother was not going to return, nor could return to fetch the daughter. All she could to is reassure the child to take the first step. It was also evident the little girl recognized her mother was slowly being pulled away and it would be up to her to do something.

How often in our spiritual lives have we felt or experienced what the little girl in the airport felt? Here we are, all suited up, dragged perhaps to a giant glow worm of a building, surrounded by strangers. Our mother or father leading the way, when suddenly they are being whisked away and we, alone, must make a decision: follow or be left behind.

As a priest I see this often in parishioners' lives and especially in priest's lives. We accept the call, the vocation. Become comfortable with our surroundings, following the lead of Our Father through His Son Jesus, when suddenly illness, a move, doubt, or spiritual aridness occupies our path, making us feel quite alone and requiring action on our part.

Once a parishioner at a parish I served came to me with such a problem. They recognized God had led them to a marital commitment to their spouse, but now it seemed their spouse had no desire to fulfill what was promised. What should they do?

Did God really intend for them to be miserable? It takes two to create a loving marriage. What if one spouse chooses to be indifferent? What choices do they have?

Such questions would perplex me as a newly ordained priest. I would always give an answer. Give reasons why God would allow such an experience. Offer points how to now handle such disappointment. I would always feel good when the person left, knowing I gave them an answer. Something to rely upon.

I don't do that anymore. I've become dumber in my old age. Some might call it wisdom though. "In the mouth of the fool is a rod for pride, but the lips of the wise preserve them." (Proverbs 14:3) My answer was primarily serving me and my conscience. It may or may not have been from the Holy Spirit.

What to do? "Trust in the Lord with all your heart, on your own intelligence do not rely. In all your ways be mindful of him, and he will make straight your paths." (Proverbs 3: 4-5) This is the "advice" I try to give now. Trust and be always mindful of Him, then take the next right step.

What happened to the little girl? Realizing her mother was slowly leaving, her voice fading; she took a leap and bounded toward her mother with wide eyes, and was received by her mother with open arms. A reunion of sorts amidst the applause of the onlookers!

She was willing not to rely on her intelligence or limited life experiences, but instead trusted, was mindful of the voice of one who had never lied before. Was her journey over?

Was this the last step of faith she would take, even with her hand firmly clasped with her mother's?

"Caution! Caution! Moving walkway is ending! Please be careful! Caution! Caution!"

"Trust in the Lord with all your heart, on your own intelligence do not rely. In all your ways be mindful of Him, and He will make straight your paths."

"Let us go forward in peace, our eyes upon heaven, the only one goal of our labors." -St. Therese of Lisieux

With an impish grin, the monk placed his weathered hand upon my elbow and whispered into my ear, "You might not want to stand there!" He pointed to what looked like 3 ton cylinder bell chimes.

I moved quickly away, as the hammer clashed onto the side of the bells, noisily announcing we no longer had to remain in the corridor silently, but could move into the dining hall to eat. In silence.

A monastery is filled with silence. Not because the monks have little to say. Be with them outside the period of silence, and you quickly realize they have much to say. And many questions of you too.

Nor is a monastery filled with silence because monks are holy. I am certain many are, but they are not silent because they are holy; they are holy because they are silent. It is in the silence God is heard.

But the monastery is also filled with bells. Noisy, loud, clashing bells. Bells announcing time to come together as a community to recognize God, or time for silence to be with the Lord. Noisy bells and silence. What an odd combination.

As a diocesan priest, my life is filled with both silence and noise. Both, I have come to understand, can be a choice.

For some, such as parents, this choice has been surrendered. Recently I baptized a child which I am not all together certain was valid because I could not hear myself speak. The child was quiet. Using warm water helps. (Did you know the Church actually encourages a priest to use warm water at a baptism? How practical! Of course, if Mother Church was truly practical, she would warn her celibate priests not to use warm water if the child, particularly a male child, is not clothed! Ahh, experience. The Mother of wisdom.)

This child was quiet but his brothers and sisters insisting on swimming in the baptismal pool (and I mean pool), and almost setting each other on fire with the baptismal candle, were raising a noisy ruckus. (I knew we were in trouble when grandpa gave little Bobby the flaming candle! Makes you wonder if grandpa had any kids? Or was he just trying to get paybacks?)

Recently I was in my own little world, my bedroom. Living alone, I make the choice to hear our Lord in silence. I was preparing for bed, without a television, phone, radio; nothing but the Lord and I, when I heard music. Loud music. Really loud. Presuming someone was in the parking lot listening to loud music, I decided to investigate.

Mustering up all my priestly authority, I chose to forgo the fuzzy Moose slippers, and put on a pair of sneakers, and headed out to the parking lot to see who was disturbing my silence with the Lord. The music became louder, but altered. Instead of the "boom, boom" of a car stereo, it sounded more live, than Memorex (dating myself!).

Cautiously I approached the parking lot, but the music was not coming from the lot. Instead it was from the cemetery adjacent to the lot. Not wanting to draw attention to myself, but speculating what was going on, I spied around the corner of the building.

Congregated around a grave were four members of a mariachi band, giving it all they had! A mariachi band, mind you. Fully dressed mariachi band! My irritation by now gave way to both amazement and amusement! What a joyous sound they were making. And I saw what I presume was family, gathered around the grave. Some crying while others were singing along.

Quietly I returned to my room, listening to the music, offering a prayer for the deceased and family; for in the noise of the music, I experienced the presence of the Lord. Although I did not understand the language of the song, I did understand the language of love being expressed. Expressed loudly!

As a diocesan priest, my life is filled with both silence and noise. Both, I have come to understand, is a choice. Sometimes a choice we make, sometimes a choice made for us. And in both, one can find the presence of God. A choice I can make for myself.

For this reason, among others, I welcome loud and noisy children to the Mass. Yes, parents should instruct their children proper Mass etiquette, but sealing up children and parents in a sound proof room (a play room) is failing to recognize the Mass is not about me receiving, it's about me giving praise and thanksgiving to God.   Both in silence and in noise!

My life, like yours, is filled with both silence and noise. God can be found in both, if we choose to hear Him.

"There are more tears shed over answered prayers than over unanswered prayers."
-St. Teresa of Avila

Picking battles

The first time it happened, I was young, but not in his eyes. Home from the seminary for the summer, I worked for a delivery company working 60-70 hour weeks. In the Liturgy of the Hours, the prayer book priests and religious daily pray, is a petition asking God's blessings on those who earn their living by the "sweat of the brow." I value those sweat filled summers as a seminarian, allowing me to understand fully what I now pray.

I had gone to a music store in the mall. I saw a condescending look in his eyes. He was my junior only by less than a few years, a teenager. It was the first time I felt out of place, and old.

"Where is the new John Denver record?" I asked. A simple question that should have elicited a simple directional answer.

"Sir," the clerk said with that look, which pierced into my mind, "I've never heard of John Denver. And we don't sell records. We sell cd's."

Afraid of asking what a "cd" is, I quickly left. This was in the mid 1980's and I was in my mid-twenties. Already the world had changed!

A few years later I was a newly ordained priest assigned to a large parish with four priests. I was the youngest with up to date knowledge...I thought. The other priests would ask what they were teaching in the seminary; what I thought we should do about this or that in the parish. Little did I understand, they were not ignorant, but were trying to include me in the ministry of the parish.

Eventually the parish had only two priests and a resident priest, and so we spread out the different responsibilities. The pastor had never had a school before, and asked me to attend the school council meetings. I presumed because of my vast knowledge of children and teachers. Now I understand, he was trying to give me a vast knowledge.

Returning from a school council meeting lasting over three hours and coming close to the verge of a war, I reported to the pastor the topic of the meeting: the dress code.

Specifically high top tennis shoes. After explaining to the pastor the differences in styles of shoes, how zebra stripped verses Converse shoes were not only a fashion statement but also a statement of the family's finances.

I explained how I had to step into the debate and explain what the parish's position should and would be on such a seemingly small matter but very imperative matter in living the Gospel in everyday life.

My pastor seemed rather befuddled about all the fuss over shoes. Having worked in poor parishes and in missions outside of the United States, he was both amused and baffled by the dress code fiasco. I, on the other hand, thought he was really "out of it" if he didn't understand the significance of such an important debate.

Smiling, he assured me that in the future, it might be more beneficial to let the parents and principal sort out dress codes and fashions, because as a priest, we don't always fully understand what is going on in society.

Giving him a condescending look, I'm sure, I countered with how a priest should be a man of culture, living in the midst of his people, guiding them through the perils of what is anti-Christian. Everything should be fodder for preaching the Gospel! He just gently smiled and went back to reading the box scores.

For the entire year the school council was focused upon dress codes. From shoes, we worked our way up: shoelaces, belts, collars on the shirts, haircuts, and earrings. I don't remember any discussion about books or curriculum, but we got the dress code into shape! For that year anyway.

Returning the next year, it had to start all over. High top tennis shoes were out! Crew socks were in! Boys wanted earrings. Girls wanted a certain book bag with a logo. Out went the old code, time to work on a new code.

I was beginning to understand what my pastor had said the year before about choosing your battles and my vast knowledge of what I thought I knew was shrinking; replaced by a vast knowledge of things I knew, I did not know. I think that is what they call getting older and wiser.

Recently I went into the mall again, into an electronics store named after what we once called an outbuilding where wood or old unused stuff were stored on the farm. Again, I could tell by the condescending look of the sales clerk's eyes I

was in trouble. He was my junior now by over 30 years.
Again I felt out of place. Old.

Simple question that should have resulted in a simple
directional answer. My question? "Where are the telephone
cords?" Answer? "Sir, telephones don't have cords!" I didn't
look, but he was probably wearing high top tennis shoes that
have come and gone and returned into fashion several times
since my early priesthood.

Getting older isn't all bad. With more limits on your time
and energy, you learn to pick your battles wisely.   I didn't
even bother explaining the history telephones to the young
man, but thanked him and found the cords on my own.
(Bottom shelf, darkest corner of the store...I got the last one!)

"Christ said, "I am the Truth"; he did not say "I am the
custom."
-St. Toribio

The Sanctuary Lamp

There are very few disconcerting things then a sanctuary lamp whose light has gone out. Few things will upset or cause parishioners to call or be certain to inform the pastor ASAP. A running toilet, a broken door, or how a Eucharistic Minister dresses inappropriately cause a certain amount of restlessness and beaten down path to the pastor's door, but nothing like a burned out sanctuary lamp.

A sanctuary lamp shines forth indicating to the church "Christ is present!" It is a beacon, like a lighthouse, summoning parishioners to come forward amidst life's rocks in adoration, to express their thanksgiving, and to pour forth their petitions. The undimmed light from a sanctuary lamp gives comfort like no other lamp in the world.

No matter what country, what language, what culture, upon entering a Catholic Church and seeing the lighted sanctuary lamp, you recognize you are home. Fumbling, bumbling, and jostled by the foreign language of the country, when you enter a Catholic Church and the language is the same. No, longer Latin but still of love. The loving Presence of our Lord proclaimed by a lamp.

Traveling one time to Europe and attempting to sleep on the way over, I had the misfortune of sitting next to two women who knew each other very well and seemed to have voluminous things to say, catching up about their daily lives. They spoke of their children, their jobs; the intimate details of their spouse, by the time they got to their health issues, ear plugs were useless. I was wide awake.

Landing in Europe, I was stunned to discover the two ladies who for eleven hours "caught up" with one another, had never met each other before sitting next to me in the plane and keeping me awake with the private details of their lives. 'How could they have spoken at such length, with such intimacy,' I thought, 'meeting for the first time?'

Exhausted, I began the new day in Europe, 8am European time, 1am my time. Touring through the day in a haze, I finally ended the very long day attending Saturday evening vigil Mass. Drained to the point of feeling ill, I stumbled into a little church to be recognized by a lighted sanctuary lamp. With renewed vigor, I kneeled and poured out my heart to the Lord about the trip, about the anxiety of traveling, about the intimate details of my life; and yes, even about the two women who, by now, I knew way too much.

I understood then how the women on the plane could communicate so freely. They found a kindred spirit, like I had found one in the remote foreign church. "...like a light shining in a dark place, until the day dawns and the morning star rises in your hearts." 2 Peter 1:19 When uncomfortable, surrounded by either darkness or apprehension, one gravitates towards such spirits and lights.

The Church states, "In accordance with traditional custom, near the tabernacle a special lamp, fueled by oil or wax, should be kept alight to indicate and honor the presence of Christ. (GIRM #316)" Jesus said, "You are the salt of the earth, but if the salt has become tasteless, how can it be made salty again? It is no longer good for anything, except to be thrown out and trampled upon. You are the light of the world...let your light shine before men..." (Matthew 5:13-14)

But what happens when our light goes out? Does the Presence of Christ no longer remain? Are we like the sanctuary lamp near the tabernacle? Christ is still present in the tabernacle when the sanctuary lamp goes out, but no one knows. There is uncertainty as to whether the light was extinguished and the Blessed Sacrament removed, or whether the light just went out. Just as there is vagueness whether Christ is present in our lives when our actions fail to show His Presence.

When the sanctuary lamp goes out, a barrage of parishioners parade to inform me. Only I and Matilda (...every church has a "Matilda" who takes care of the candles), have knowledge where the sanctuary lamp replacements are and lights it. When a fellow parishioner, family member, or our own "sanctuary lamp" grows dim or out, do we have the same concern? The same angst?

Sitting or kneeling before a Tabernacle with an unlighted sanctuary lamp is disconcerting. We "know" Christ is "probably" present, but tentative whether He is really sacramentally Present. It just doesn't seem right, but nor does faith without good works. (James 2:17)

The Church goes on to say, "In no way should all the other things prescribed by law concerning the reservation of the Most Holy Eucharist be forgotten." (GIRM #317) Like a sanctuary lamp, forgotten until it is absent, so too the Light of Christ in our lives, often over looked, until absent.

There are very few disconcerting things then a sanctuary lamp whose light has gone out. Whether in the church sanctuary or in our lives.

"To keep a lamp burning we have to keep putting oil in it" - *Mother Teresa*

The Success of our Failures

Slowly they came forward. Years of pastoral experience.
The wisdom etched on their faces was revealed in the evening
light shining through the chapel windows. As the prayers of
the Church were prayed over them, a priest, many years their
younger, placed his hands on their bowed heads.

Extending their hands, palms down, the junior priest
anointed the backsides of their hands with holy oil of the
infirmed, praying for healing. Healing of body, mind, and soul.
Healing of the past so the present might be faced with
renewed vigor.

Yearly the priests of the diocese gather for a retreat.
These retreats are wondrous events of sharing between the
generations. The older priests tell the younger what it was
like in the old days. The days when "associates" were
"assistants" and when the assistants were in fact lower in
ranking than the housekeeper or the pastor's pet.

Some of the stories are simply of far distant times, such as
the pastor who expected the assistant to clean the fish he had
caught or pluck the feathers from the donated live chicken.
But some of the stories make you wonder how the church
survived, or more importantly, how the pastor's dog survived.
Such as the time an assistant was walking through the house
late at night, only to squarely find the droppings of the
pastor's dog under his bare foot. Or the time the assistant let
the dog loose to be reprimanded by the pastor for such
inattention, only to have the assistant cry, "You care about

the dog more than me!" to which the pastor was unable to reply in charity.

But then, not to be out done, the younger priests, always respectfully, advise the older priests how difficult they have it now with the many new expectations of a priest. The amount of travel, technological expertise needed, and how they are becoming pastors so much younger. Stories today however, seem pale in comparison to yesterday!

The older priests generally smile knowingly, never telling the younger priests, they too were overwhelmed by these pressures, although through different circumstances, the pressures were the same: that is to proclaim the Gospel of Jesus Christ while still trying to retain one's balance in life.

Watching this interchange this past year at our priest retreat, I was struck by the manner in which the conversation played out. I saw the older priests not only mentor, for mentoring is where a more knowledgeable person helps a less experienced person by providing answers or support. No what I saw was nurturing.

Nurturing offers answers to questions, but most of all creates the atmosphere of a father, providing a safe environment for a younger priest to not only ask questions, but to express emotions and even to be unsuccessful safely.

Struggling in a new parish, I remember a nurturing moment. Meeting with a group of priests, I shared my long litany of struggles in my new parish. To sum it up, I felt unsuccessful. I was floored when an older priest, pushing all my struggles and complaints aside, simply said, "Don't be afraid to fail."

"What do you mean, fail?" I asked. He went on to share a pastoral experience with me how he felt he had failed in a particular parish. How the experience changed him for the better. While he would not want to experience it again, we knew he was in the right place at the right time. It was God's providential plan for both him and the parish. His "failure" was necessary for both he and the parish.

His statement altered my view. I went forward now unafraid to fail. Looking at the cross, I know failure is sometimes success.

Recently I was able to visit that priest as he was recovering from major surgery. Humbly I anointed the backside of his hands for the Anointing of the Sick, forgiving his sins and praying for full recovery. He was in pain by the failure of his body now in old age. Eventually his body will fail him completely, as will ours. Only then will we fully comprehend the success of our failures.

"You must ask God to give you power to fight against the sin of pride which is your greatest enemy – the root of all that is evil, and the failure of all that is good. For God resists the proud."-St. Vincent de Paul

174

The aftermath of the Mass, Part I

They come out of the gates either in full gallop and I feel like I am drinking out of a fire hose, or they stampede like a herd of turtles, walkers and all. The conversations vary from the slapping of high or low fives to a clarification of a theological point; from the knee hug of a child to a grieving hug of a widow. The gate is the church doors. The time is the conclusion of Mass.

I like the new translation. It has slowed me down. The words are more visual. Yes, I understand there are words we don't always use. Yes, some are cumbersome, but we will get used to it. Think of the Lord's Prayer. How often do we say "thee" and "thou" in our everyday language? Yet, there they are: "Hollowed be Thy name." How often do we even say "hollowed?"

It is the new endings of the Mass I appreciate the most. Hearing the new dismissal rites, I picture Christ assuring the apostles as He is about to leave them again and ascend into heaven. "You are to be my witnesses in Jerusalem...yes, even to the ends of the earth." He sends them forth with power and authority.

The new translation offers the same muscle: "Go forth, the Mass is ended." Or "Go and announce the Gospel of the Lord." And finally, "Go in peace, glorifying the Lord by your life." This last one really sets one forth on the right foot!

It is after Mass the church gathers and recognizes the Lord whom they have received in word and in flesh. Whether in a gathering place, a foyer, or simply the parking lot, the after Mass crowd is truly the assembly of the faithful. Where both friend and foe meet. It is a gateway.

"Well?" She forcefully asked. "Well, what are you going to make me do?" Her name was Esther (name has been changed to protect me) and I just concluded celebrating my first Mass on a Sunday as the new pastor. (I have lots of new parish stories...I can't seem to keep a job or parish) Esther was seated behind a small desk selling a local grocery store certificates of which the parish would receive a portion of the proceeds.

I never liked the practice of selling things in the back of the church. The occasional bake sale was okay, but a regular shopping mall always reminded me of what Jesus spoke of in the Temple as a "den of thieves." Matthew 21:13. Thieves are a little harsh, but sometimes on a given Sunday you might have popcorn sales, cookie sales, gift certificate sales, and Altar Society or Knights of Columbus sales. Thieves are too strong, but it can be a gauntlet of good causes.

Esther was waiting for an answer; an answer from me, the new pastor. An answer, I knew as the new pastor, Esther would not like.

The former pastor had requested all transactions after Mass be conducted outside the church foyer. The vestibule was very small and once you allow one group, everyone should be able to. Even though the certificates were helping the parish, in my head I knew the former pastor was right. Too little space for table, chair, and Esther.

Looking at Esther, I realized I could have, should have her move, but knew the conclusion of the Mass I gave would never be reality if I did, that is, "Go in peace!" This was a test. The former pastor told me when he left there were many challenges the parish was facing and in his naivety, many of the challenges was created by him! He realized he was too strict.

I knew the feeling. Every parent does. The raising of the last child is very different from the parenting techniques for the first child. For priests, parishes are like children. In our first pastorate we often go overboard in discipline and doing it the "right way." After five or six parishes, you worry less about the "right way," and you just go for the way that will best build up the body of Christ and keep you sane. This means sometimes being smart where you choose to draw a line in the sand.

"Of course, you can stay right where you are Esther!" I said. Her smile lit up the entire small foyer of the church. I knew I made the right decision. Cluttered church foyer? Yes. But a very happy church in peace indeed!

The aftermath of the Mass, Part 2

After Mass, the flow of parishioners flow both ways: parishioners leaving Mass and coming to the next Mass. The flow out is likened to drinking out of a fire hose. There are so many parishioners, all at once, and you want to say something to each one.

One particular Sunday I was substituting at a parish and greeting the parishioners after Mass in the foyer. I felt like a weather vane being turned from direction to direction, trying to greet them all

After the onslaught of people I begin to make my way back to the sacristy when I heard, "Father, do you have a minute?" I stopped and said I did. It was a young mother with a small child in tow. "My son has something to tell you." she said. I stood, waiting for the son to perhaps give me a picture he had drawn on the front of the bulletin during my homily (see someone does read or at least use them!), or perhaps he had a great theological question such as do dogs go to heaven. (Of course they do! As Will Rogers said, "If dogs don't go to heaven, I want to go where they go!")

Tearfully he blurted out, "I'm sorry!" Confused, I asked why. He was unable to speak, so I looked to his mother. Determinedly she explained how the boy had misbehaved at church and she wanted him to learn his lesson by apologizing to me.

No problem, I thought. Good lesson to make amends, especially to the one person at Mass who is in persona Christi, the priest. But I was taken aback by what she said next. "I'm not above humiliating my children when they act up in Mass, and make them apologize to the priest." Quite shaken and unable to respond, I mumbled something like, "That's okay." and quickly moved into the sacristy.

My shock turned to anger in the sacristy. I felt used. I realize raising children is the most difficult task in the world and the mother was doing what she thought was best, but humiliation is never God's way. Thinking of how I could have responded differently, I wish I would have said something like, "I am sorry you misbehaved at Mass, but Jesus loves you very much and wants to show His love to you and your mother at Mass. Try to be better next time." Many other lines went through my head of what I could have said, should have said, but did not say.

After mentally finger pointing at the mother whose determination to create good behavior in a child at the expense of damaging a relationship between her son and the Lord or the office of the priesthood, I began to think about some of my dumb moments as a "parent."

I remember the time I insisted the bag on the unconsecrated host be firmly zipped in the sacristy with Alvin my sacristan. Making sure the hosts did not dry out or became stale was more important to me than appreciating his time and effort to serve me at a very early Mass.

I can only now imagine what this war veteran thought of me making such an issue over zip lock bags. Thankfully the

Lord intervened and allowed me reparation many years later when I unexpectedly stumbled upon Alvin in a nursing home and I was able to give him the final sacraments. Zip lock bags were the furthest thing I cared about then.

Or the time I maintained my associate should hang the chasubles and stoles in a certain manner so they would not wrinkle. Signs. Lots of Post It notes fixed it! Until he told me he was tired of all of those little Post It notes everywhere. So I changed. I began to use legal sheets! The stoles were smooth, but our relationship became wrinkled. I often wonder what this young priest (now 15 years older) remembers of me. I probably cross his mind every time he uses a Post It note!

I hope the mother of the wayward son learns the lessons I've learned the hard way. We are both parents, both trying to do the right things for our children, but sometimes the wrong way. I finally had to keep reminding myself: 'Minister to people, not things!'

Being a parent is hard work, and we make mistakes. Our children will remember our mistakes for sure, but more importantly they will remember how we tried to make amends. It's a flow both ways, for someday our children will have children too, then they will look at us very differently, with understanding eyes.

I suspect our Heavenly Father understands too!

Conclusion

I am always amazed at the generosity and gratitude of God's People. While the names and circumstances in these stories have been changed or altered to protect privacy, my admiration and appreciation of the support the People of God has given me both in my priesthood and in my writing remains unchanged and unaltered.

Thank you for allowing me to share the gift that was freely given to me. (See Matthew 10:8)

Mary, mother of priests. Pray for us.

Father Ken VanHaverbeke
Diocese of Wichita

*The proceeds of this book will be donated to **The Center of Hope** in Wichita, Kansas. The Center of Hope, sponsored by the Sisters Adorers of the Blood of Christ (ASC), provides emergency financial support to individuals and families in Wichita who may not otherwise qualify for other social service programs. In many cases, the Center of Hope provides a last hope for their clients. For more information about the Center of Hope go to www.centerofhopeinc.org.*

"Believe what you read; Preach what you believe; Practice what you preach" The Ordination Rite